PEAK HIGHER ED

PEAK HIGHER ED

How to Survive the Looming Academic Crisis

BRYAN ALEXANDER

JOHNS HOPKINS UNIVERSITY PRESS | *Baltimore*

First printed in the United States of America on acid-free paper
2 4 6 8 9 7 5 3 1

Johns Hopkins University Press
2715 North Charles Street
Baltimore, Maryland 21218
www.press.jhu.edu

Library of Congress Cataloging-in-Publication Data is available.

A catalog record for this book is available from the British Library.

ISBN 978-1-4214-5470-2 (hardcover)
ISBN 978-1-4214-5471-9 (ebook)

EU GPSR Authorized Representative
LOGOS EUROPE, 9 rue Nicolas Poussin,
17000, La Rochelle, France
E-mail: Contact@logoseurope.eu

Dedicated to those who fell, but live in me still: Amy, Bernie, Carl, Charles, Cliff, Earle, George, Jenny, John, Mike, Natalie, Nelson, Oink, Rob, Shel, and Tomak.

Beneath these darkening clouds lies an increasingly economically and institutionally denuded landscape, vulnerable to landslide. Following years of radical decrease in state support for universities and corresponding increase in tuition costs and student indebtedness, many universities now seem near a financial breaking point.

—Professor Gabriel Winant,
University of Chicago

For three generations, the national aspiration to "college for all" shaped America's economy and culture, as most high-school graduates took it for granted that they would earn a degree. That consensus is now collapsing in the face of massive student debt, underemployed degree-holders and political intolerance on campus.

—Doug Belkin, *Wall Street Journal*

American higher education is not just staring into the abyss—it has already fallen into it.

—Donald Earl Collins, Professorial Lecturer
at American University in Washington, DC

CONTENTS

ACKNOWLEDGMENTS

This book represents the outcome of many, many conversations. To name some discussants, I thank Stephen Aguilar-Millan, Nate Angell, Arindam Basu, Karen Bellnier, Doug Belshaw, Bill Benzon, Donald Clark, Karen Costa, Emory Craig, Andrew Curry, Kim DeBacco, Mark DeFusco, Ashley Finley, Maya Georgieva, Arturo E. Hernandez, Krista Hiser, Jarek Janio, Phil Katz, Steven Kaye, Joshua Kim, Paul LeBlanc, Cliff Lynch, Anna Mills, Rod "The Militant Optimist" Murray, John O'Brien, Jo Ellen Parker, Rick Perlstein, Kaelynn Reid, Mike Roy, Mark Salisbury, Daita Serghi, Gary Stocker, Alex Usher, Ben Wildavsky, Ian Wilhelm, and Mark Corbett Wilson. Early readers showed great stamina and patience: James Dator, John Hollenbeck, Tom Lairson, Ruben Puentedura, Mark Rush, and Peter Shea.

Interview subjects Michael Clarke, Danielle Douglas-Gabriel, and Bill McKibben were very generous with their time.

Many people in online spaces contributed to making this book possible. All supporters on Patreon were helpful, including those who energetically talked me through key ideas, such as Brett Boessen, Patricia Clay, Steve Foerster, Joanna Richardson, carrie saarinen, Vanessa Vaile, and Ed Webb. Members of the extraordinary Future Trends Forum community helped similarly, almost too many to mention, but folks like Lisa Durff, Tom Haymes, John Hollenbeck, Roxann Riskin, George Station, and the excellent Wesson Radomsky stand out for their thoughtfulness and kindness. Chris Newfield and his Facebook group were good discussants and sounding boards. The pages that follow cite some Forum sessions by name, but our years of weekly discussion inform every paragraph.

I owe thanks to colleagues at Georgetown University. Faculty and staff in the Learning, Design, and Technology program put up with my odd questions and rants. Students offered good feedback for elements of this book. The Lauinger Library was an invaluable resource for writing the chapters which follow as its reference librarians answered my barrages of questions and interlibrary loan did heroic work in finding all kinds of documents.

Groups of friends helped see this volume come to pass. Steven Kaye and Jesse Walker kindly bore up under my questions and supplied me with stories. The Paradigm project was a powerful resource for optimism in dark times, notably its leader David Scobey and the whole remarkable crew. *Higher Education Inquirer* discussants Keil Dumsch, Glen McGee, and Dahn Shaulius shared information, helped hone points in this book, and deepened its arguments through daily conversation. You all have been among the most keen-eyed observers of peak higher education. The Last Humans movement helped with the big questions: Trent Batson, Randy Bass (Randy, I owe chapter six to you), and Phil Long. My colleagues at the Association of Professional Futurists have provided many conversations and resources. Doug Shapiro and the National Student Clearinghouse team were invaluable resources.

Greg Britton, generous editor and networker extraordinaire, saw the potential in this book when it was just a few blog posts and helped guide it to completion. He has survived three books with me now and is a fine friend.

My brave wife was very patient with me as I furiously typed, read, rambled, fumed, ranted, and brooded on this book's subject for years. You have all of my love.

ABBREVIATIONS

AGI	Artificial general intelligence
AI	Artificial intelligence
CDC	Centers for Disease Control and Prevention, United States
DEI	Diversity, equity, and inclusion
EV	Electric vehicle
GDP	Gross domestic product
HBCU	Historically black colleges and universities
HSI	Hispanic serving institution
IP	Intellectual property
IT	Information technology
LLM	Large language model, a type of AI
NCES	National Center for Education Statistics
OLLI	Osher Lifelong Learning InstituteXReXtended Reality, a synthesis of virtual reality (VR) and augmented reality (AR)

PEAK HIGHER ED

INTRODUCTION

Have American colleges and universities passed their peak? Has the nation's higher education system become overbuilt for its purposes?

To ask such questions is provocative, deliberately so. It might seem odd or perverse to raise them. After all, American higher education is a global leader. Our top universities routinely score well in international rankings. Academic research is world-class in a variety of ways, from sheer output to the extensive number of Nobel Prize winners and patents held, clearly producing an astonishing amount of knowledge. Our pedagogy is distinct, perhaps unique, in its emphasis on student support, care, empowerment, and engagement. We boast thousands of campuses with an astonishing variety of institutional types: religious, public, liberal arts, military, arts, technological, community college, research university, and more. More than ten million students enroll in these colleges and universities. Out of that group, more than one million students journeyed from around the world to the United States for postsecondary study in the academic year 2023–24. Our richest colleges and universities boast vast endowments to the count of tens of billions of dollars. Surely the nation's higher education sector is excellent and has never been more brilliant.[1]

Yet we have recently seen the sector plateau or shrink in some vital ways, after generations of growth. The total number of enrolled students grew very well from the early 1980s until 2011, peaking at 18,077,303, according to federal data, whereupon the number shrank every year for a decade, both before and during the COVID-19 pandemic. During that declining decade, popular views of higher education soured. At the same time, the total number of campuses shrank. The total number of all postsecondary enterprises peaked at 7,253 in the academic year 2012–13, dropping down to 5,916 in 2020–21, according to federal data. Title IV campuses fell from 4,726 to 3,931, with two-year colleges falling from 1,700 to 1,294 while four-year schools dropped from 3,026 to 2,637.[2]

If that decline continues for another decade or more, if the forces which caused it continue over the next several years without mitigation, then we might experience:

- Higher education shrinking as a whole. The number of campuses, students, faculty, staff, and programs declines
- Popular opinion about academia souring further. Public opposition rises, ranging from neglect to threats or even to property damage and violence
- Total enrollment numbers falling
- Governmental support receding financially. Alternatively, some governments (federal, state, local) increase their interventions into colleges and universities, seeking to alter a range of processes and functions, from curriculum to hiring, student discipline and accreditation. Colleges and universities having a diminished impact on the great issues of the day, from social justice to climate change, artificial intelligence to geopolitics
- People experiencing personal damage as fewer of us pursue dreams of higher learning, and as academic faculty and staff see their careers blighted. Society arguably suffers as a result

"If" is a keyword here. This is a book about a possibility. It describes a scenario, one story of a future which could occur and seems to be emerging right now. Its shape and details are based on recent history and current developments, analyzed by years of research and feedback, developed using the futures method of scenario construction. This is, in short, one potential future for American higher education. In the following chapters, we will investigate how American colleges and universities could change if we continue to operate in a post-peak fashion. This is, necessarily, a work of informed speculation, grounded in documentary evidence drawn from the present and recent past.

In short, this book is a work of futures thinking. The futures field (also known as foresight, forecasting, and the strategic foresight profession, among other synonyms) offers many intellectual tools and frameworks to apprehend possible futures. From those methods, the present volume uses scenario thinking, developing and exploring the implications of a particular future, itself based on current trends. Scenarios are rich but limited methods for exploring the future. Their power comes from the capacity of storytelling to engage the imagination, as well as the human predisposition toward role play. We can envision ourselves in the scenario's world (remember the etymological link between "scenario" and "scene," "scene setting"), thinking through what we might do. The more detailed a scenario, the more we can explore and stretch our own futuring muscles. We can ground those details in recent history and the present, documenting how higher education and its social contexts change and develop. We might think of crafting a scenario like this as a kind of in media res writing, as Columbia University economic historian Adam Tooze describes: being caught in the middle of an unfolding process, seeking to glimpse its arc in time. As such, we invite the reader to participate in this act of imagination: to think through how peak higher education could unfold, to question its details, and to wonder how your work, your institution(s), and your lives might change should it come to pass. This is a topic for institutions as a whole, for the entire sector, as well as for individuals within the space.[3]

One limitation of scenario work is that a given scenario represents only a single future built upon one or several driving forces. They typically do not "come true" in the sense of accurately describing the world to come as a whole. Instead, some scenarios accurately forecast some aspects of the world at certain times. In these situations, they identify one strand of a braided time. Their real strength comes from showing users (or readers) how to rethink their future under a given set of conditions.

Users (or readers) can then apply that rethinking and forecasting ability to related scenarios and situations, increasing their readiness and flexibility. It is my hope that the peak higher education scenario this book explores will assist readers in this general goal. It is my fervent hope that American academia does not fall further from its peak, but I fear it is likely that at least parts of the sector will. Working through this scenario may prove all too helpful in those cases.

Does this book offer a declinist narrative? In anticipation of doom-mongering charges, I state at the outset, yes, to some extent, much of what follows describes a story (scenario) of one postsecondary system literally declining, falling back from a historic peak. In nonprofit or public policy terms, we can consider this story to be one of a long-provided service which now exceeds, to a decisive degree, the needs it was designed to serve. In economic language, we could view peak higher ed as an instance of classic supply and demand, where demand falls and a painful market correction follows. I do not offer this scenario out of glee or sadism, but to help academics and those others concerned with higher education to think ahead more effectively. To ignore negative possibilities because they are unpleasant would be futurist malpractice.

Yet it is important to recall that a story about the entire sector of American postsecondary education is a broad, macro-level one, and that once we shift our focus to a smaller scale, we will see a much more complex picture. We could say that peak higher education, like the future in William Gibson's famous observation, is unevenly distributed. Institutions occupying the reputational heights and possessed of great wealth tend to survive downturns unscathed, or even prosper, while damage tends to hit other strata within the broader landscape: lower-ranked liberal arts colleges, state universities with open enrollment or close to it, strongly religious institutions suffering from many pressures, including a social trend of secularization. American higher education is very disorganized, complex, and varied—a perfect mess, in David F. Labaree's felicitous phrase. And within those strata, some campuses will succeed brilliantly due to a mix of their own decisions, their particular situation, and good luck. Peak higher education is a big-picture story and, like all macro narratives, will be present at meso and micro levels to varying degrees.[4]

There is one further caveat to offer for the decline narrative. In this book, we also discuss ways that colleges and universities can rethink and revise how these institutions operate in a way that rebuilds the sector, attracting new levels of interest and support. *Peak Higher Ed* describes a statistical peak from which we are at increasing risk of falling, but "peak" also refers to exceptionally positive performance and experience. The many stresses our sector faces may drive us to reimagine what a campus is and how it functions in ways that improve the situations of all concerned, from students and staff to faculty and senior leaders. Simply put, one peak may inspire another.

As an extended exploration of a future of higher education scenario, the present book is a sequel to two previous volumes published by Johns Hopkins University Press. My 2023 title, *Universities on Fire*, was an extended exploration of a single trend, rather than a scenario: escalating climate change, and as one set of results, its many emerging impacts on colleges and universities. It broke down those impacts across several domains: the physical plant of a campus, academic research, teaching, and community relations. That book's predecessor, *Academia Next* (2020), took a broader view, using both trend and scenario analysis to grapple with higher education's future. Indeed, it offered a group of scenarios and dozens of trends across domains as diverse as macroeconomics, virtual reality, and demographics. One of those scenarios, briefly described, is the focus of the present volume. *Academia Next*, like this book, focused on American higher education, while *Universities on Fire* examined the entire world of postsecondary education. Taken together, the three books are a trilogy, each taking a different tack in envisioning what might come next for academia.

In the present volume, we begin by exploring the past decade of post-peak higher education, grounding our speculative scenario in real-world evidence. Chapter one identifies the historical moment of peak, then describes what happened afterward to colleges and universities through to the present day. We discuss the available data from multiple sources, teasing out the contours of peak, establishing limitations to what we can currently know. On a qualitative level, we explore some reasons behind that decline in all its complexity and unevenness, from student debt to changing political attitudes. We start to outline various responses that some academic institutions and other actors in the postsecondary space have given.

Building on that historical and present-day background, chapter two carries peak higher education forward into the next decade. This section offers the scenario proper, building up a model of how colleges and universities might change if the forces underlying peak persist and if others join them. We develop those forces, examining demographics, institutional finances, worsening public attitudes, political challenges, and competitors, before pondering some potential political side effects.

In chapter three, we examine one crucial and, I believe, underdiscussed implication to peak higher education, which is the breaking up of a multigenerational consensus around the importance of postsecondary learning. America has recently committed itself to the idea of "college for all," a stance which has been apparent across our society, from reshaping K-12 toward general college preparation to the emergence of college and university business models resting on ever-increasing enrollment. We explore that idea as it rose over time with a survey of its historical background. Then we uncover how that commitment has frayed and possibly shattered in recent years, based in part on the evidence of declining student numbers. Cultural and political attitudes toward postsecondary education have also shifted, with increasingly partisan divides setting in over the perceived benefits of higher education. The end of college for all, or its transmutation into "college for some," suggests further pressure on higher education to slide below its peak.

In the next three chapters, we broaden our analytical lens to situate the peak scenario in the face of three massive challenges. Chapter four explores how artificial intelligence (AI) might impact higher education in the context of wider social transformation. Multiple possibilities open up on this score, which might further the peak model, including a degradation in academia's reputation based on the perception that students learn little, as well as the potential for learners to choose learning via AI, relying on tutorbots and other software, over a far more expensive college experience. At the same time, AI offers opportunities for academic institutions to transform their work in ways that could support their pedagogical, research, and service purposes. This section updates and expands on two chapters in *Academia Next*—"Augmented Campus" and "Siri, Tutor Me."

Chapter five returns to *Universities on Fire* by examining the intersections between the climate crisis and higher education. It identifies several ways the many implications of global warming could further the peak model. We begin by outlining the major domains within which global warming impacts colleges and universities: physical damage to campuses and populations through storms, floods, aridification, and other natural pressures; changes to our environment due to impacts on ecosystems, including new disease patterns and alterations to campus flora and fauna; and the many implications of human responses to climate change, including the political and cultural. Next, we identify multiple levels of academic engagement, starting with reforming our physical campuses and operations, then changing our research and teaching missions, followed by community engagement at local and global levels. There are several ways climate stresses and academic responses could further push higher education below peak. I also argue that academia could avoid the worst implications of the scenario if it engages seriously with climate change.

We then examine an even deeper future in chapter six, where I offer a model of an emerging conflict between attitudes toward the next century. One developing school of thought argues that humanity should double down on innovation and progress, devoting more energy to continuing the many advances we have enjoyed from the several industrial revolutions. In contrast, another way of thinking holds that civilization should instead turn to mitigating those revolutions' harms and must reduce humanity's footprint on many levels. This "battle for the future" is unfolding throughout society and clearly connects with colleges and universities. Will academia continue to embrace our role in nurturing and producing new knowledge, as well as remaining wedded to both institutional and macroeconomic growth? Or will the postsecondary sector experience a further shrinkage as society moves away from expansion and an inherited sense of progress? Taken together, the reader might see chapters four through six as variations on the peak higher education scenario and the different iterations and forms it might take.

In chapters seven and eight, we return our focus to colleges and universities in the present, looking into their options in the face of the preceding. Chapter seven models how academics and our institutions could adapt to the peak scenario in a mindset of managed decline. This is one dark ending to our book, envisioning a further decline. In contrast, chapter eight offers strategies for how academia might attempt to return to growth or at least sustainability. This conclusion offers a second sense for "peak higher education": a qualitative rather than quantitative meaning along the lines of peak performance or peak experience. This optimistic path supposed that our creative responses to a statistical peak could yield a far more effective and humane academic sector.

While each chapter makes a distinct argument or offers a single vision, they often link to each other. Chapter eight stands in opposition to seven, for example, while both are responses to the grand challenges depicted in four through six. Chapters one through three, in a sense, offer three cuts through one scenario, adjusted in time and by culture. I invite readers to make their own connections between these segments.

Over their linear sequence, these chapters gradually reach a very ambitious level, starting with details of one nation's academic sector in a short period before ultimately wrestling with the fate of global civilization over more than a century to come. At the same time, and perhaps gratefully, the reader should otherwise be prepared for some restrictions of scope. The primary temporal window looks ahead a decade or two, to 2035–40, although the forces we address extend beyond that, climate change alone being a multi-century process. In spatial terms, this book focuses on the postsecondary ecosystem within the United States, partly to keep the discussion to a single volume, but also in recognition of American academia's diversity and global stature at present. This nation's sector is, as mentioned, internationally very influential. It is also quite different from higher education in the rest of the world, and requires distinct treatment. That said, while the United States grapples with peak higher education, other nations may experience their own versions of it. For example, the university sectors of Australia, New Zealand, Germany, Canada, and the United Kingdom are all experiencing challenges to their sustainability. The social and civilizational forces we will describe impinge on the whole world, including all postsecondary sectors, not just the American one. While each nation's system has, of course, a distinct nature, there are some common threads connecting them. Consider these passages describing multiple nations' academic challenges, starting with continental Europe:

> In many countries a demographic decline in enrolment in tertiary education has already begun, notably in Eastern European countries like Lithuania, Slovakia, Bulgaria, Poland, Estonia, Czechia and Hungary, where enrolment numbers in 2020 made up between 85% and 78% of the numbers in 2015.

Great Britain may face something similar:

> An unforeseen drop in demand for higher education in England could prove to be a "nightmare" for universities. . . .
>
> A report written by Higher Education Policy Institute president Bahram Bekhradnia finds that previous estimates of 350,000 more students by 2035 are now unrealistic after recent drops in the participation rate, casting doubt on institutions' ability to grow their way out of their current financial troubles.
>
> While the country's 18-year-old population has swelled since 2020 and is projected to reach its highest point this century in 2030, this has not yet translated into a big increase in student numbers, the paper highlights.
>
> Instead, 2023 and 2024 saw the first declines in the application rate for 18-year-olds after steady increases since 2012, as interest in attending university stagnated among young people, which, the paper suggests, is "largely unprecedented in the past three decades."

Or consider Australia, where University of Adelaide Vice-Chancellor Peter Høj said, "We've got to be realistic about a time where the demand for Australian education is not as pronounced as it is now."[5]

Shrinking demand, decreasing interest, financial troubles, demographic shifts: all of this should be familiar to observers of the United States academic world and will be major themes in the pages which follow.

Now, within that narrow focus on American higher education, I hope to address the entire ecosystem. Research universities, community colleges, state universities, military academies, liberal arts colleges, public and private, religious and otherwise, are all involved in the peak higher education scenario in varying ways. All too often, discourse around higher education focuses on only a part of this world, typically a slice of the elite. It is vital, just, and more accurate to consider the whole. At the same time, this book maintains this focus on institutions of higher education; it will not have space to consider informal learning at length.

I hope that this wide-ranging futures account will be useful to anyone in that academic world as they consider what might occur next and their role in that transformation, from professors to students, presidents to staff members. I think this book will also contribute to discussions about higher education's future being held in sites and organizations adjacent to and having an interest in colleges and universities, such as foundations, state governments, companies making products and services for the academic market, policymakers, and voters. Members of the "GLAM" sector may find this of some utility as well: galleries, libraries, archives, and museums, as well as other cultural heritage institutions.

I must acknowledge the important political context of writing this book. I conducted most of its final research, composition, editing, and revision through the years 2023–25, and during this period, many nations experienced various forms of heightened stress on their colleges and universities, not to mention their entire societies. Some governments, such as Hungary's and China's, exerted increasing pressure on campus administrations, curricula, and research. Nations at war saw students, faculty, and staff injured, killed, or driven into exile, from Ukraine to Lebanon,

Israel, Gaza, and Sudan. Students played key roles in protests and unrest. Some observers saw a rising tide of authoritarian politics advancing worldwide. The horrific term "scholasticide" reappeared. Natural disasters exacerbated by climate change struck academics on and off campus from Mexico to Pakistan. Ripple effects from these events spread across other postsecondary institutions as campuses hosted refugees, made or broke partnerships, reconsidered curricular offerings, rethought international units, and responded to governmental policies.

We can think of these multiple, connecting events as a "polycrisis," and its ripples reached American higher education, of course. Our sector was subjected to many other domestic political forces during this period. Some state governments attempted to pass laws impacting faculty governance, diversity programs, student expression, and curricula; several succeeded. Political activists of various stripes called for platforming or deplatforming speakers, revising curricula, and changing the demographic or political makeup of campus faculty, students, and staff. Pro-Palestinian protests roiled mostly elite campuses. Congressional hearings led to the ignominious exit of several elite university presidents. Some campuses expanded, then reduced, their diversity initiatives and programs. Academic institutions were clearly sites of contested politics, and some academics were energetic actors off campus.[6]

At the presidential level, Democrat Joe Biden sought to forgive student loans at an unprecedented level, opposed by court rulings and the other political party, while the Republican vice-presidential candidate (who later assumed that office) channeled Richard Nixon to proclaim "the professors are the enemy." J. D. Vance also recommended that "we have to honestly and aggressively attack the universities in this country." A leading Republican think tank published a book-length plan for a new administration to follow, including multiple direct and indirect moves against postsecondary institutions, from cracking down on campus diversity, equity, and inclusion (DEI) efforts to ending the Department of Education, from punishing academics for allowing access to online pornography to launching a series of new academies. In 2024 and 2025, as a candidate and then president, Donald Trump urged multiple attacks on higher education from various directions, including redoing the accreditation system, rooting out DEI and Marxism, taxing endowments, and more. As of this writing, Trump has launched an extensive campaign against colleges and universities. This includes, but is not limited to, an effort to close the Department of Education, cut billions of dollars in grant funding to research universities, investigate dozens of institutions for multiple alleged harms, challenge incoming international students, and intervene in some universities' internal processes. His other policy ideas (and "concepts of plans") would impact colleges and universities in other ways, such as conducting a massive deportation campaign that detained some academics and their family members, while ramping up a new Cold War with China with all kinds of implications for international campuses, research, and enrollment. As I write these words, many American academics appear filled with anxiety, uncertainty, or dread.[7]

We will address this contemporary political environment throughout the following chapters, as it would be foolish to ignore it. The various elements of polycrisis foreign and domestic has impacted and will impact the next several years of American higher education (chapters two and three), shapes our national response to AI and climate change (chapters four and five), inflects increasingly divergent ideas about progress (chapter six), accelerates or restrains efforts to redesign our institutions (chapters seven and eight), and generally has the capacity to affect nearly every academic endeavor.

I want to draw the reader's attention to this context here for several reasons. First, the political environment played a significant role in the making of this book, due to my personal exposure to some of the issues, as well as my own limited activism around the 2024 election and its aftermath. Professionally, throughout that year, I hosted a series of events to help academics prepare for a then-possible second Trump administration, from leading a sustained, open, and online reading of Project 2025 to hosting a series of live video scenario exercises to blogging forecasts. I continued my several years of trying to encourage academics to take more climate action. Since the election and installation of the new government, I have scrambled to share information, to support those who need it, all while attempting to minimize risks. The blizzard of executive actions, public statements, policy changes, and bureaucratic wilding does not generally bode well for many of us laboring in colleges and universities. There exist threats of various kinds to a good number of us. To some extent, publicly criticizing Republican actions entails risk. The reader may find traces of such a mindset in this text.

Second, the chaotic nature of a second Trump administration makes forecasting more difficult, given the president's inconsistencies when it comes to policies. In the futures field, we speak of difficult-to-anticipate events as wild cards or black swans. This government seems to possess a full deck of wild cards in addition to a well-stocked swan menagerie and is enthusiastically dealing all of them out to the world. We will try to connect these short-term signals to longer-term trends as far as is possible.

Third, it may well be that the second Trump administration pushes American higher education downslope past peak. The first such administration occupied four years of post-peak academia and helped worsen things in some ways. The second seems well-positioned to do even more. We will address this potential in the chapters to come.

On an even more personal note, I first started investigating the peak higher education idea in 2012, during the Obama presidency. At the time, I was working for the National Institute for Technology in Liberal Education, researching the potential implications of emerging technology and inter-institutional collaboration for American small colleges. Looking into 2012's national enrollment data as part of my scanning practice, I found the National Student Clearinghouse reporting that student numbers had declined. This surprised me as the nation's higher education enrollment growth had steadily increased for decades, as far as I knew.

That age of academic growth defined my own academic career. I started at the University of Michigan as a first-year student in 1985 and took my PhD there in 1995, seeing that large campus (actually two campuses, plus a connected state system) grow. I taught literature and composition at Centenary College until 2002, watching (and to a small degree helping) that campus build back from a very challenging period. From 2002 to 2013, I worked for the National Institute for Technology in Liberal Education (NITLE) by focusing on helping hundreds of small liberal arts colleges collaborate and grapple with technology. Some struggled, while the elite thrived. The 2008 Great Recession shocked higher education badly, and while a kind of recovery gradually and unevenly occurred, it introduced the possibility that colleges and universities were more vulnerable than they seemed beforehand. And in 2012, enrollment had dipped. That statistical note opened up a possibility. A small decline could have been just statistical noise or a fluke caused by an unusual factor or factors, to be sure, but it might also represent a break in the long-running trend of burgeoning student numbers. What might that break lead to?

Extrapolation is a basic, sometimes clumsy way of projecting a trend in the futures field. One takes several data points from related metrics and then extends them forward in a line, turning one-dimensional observations into a story. However, extrapolation often falls apart in the face of reality, which tends to be messier and more complex than a straight line, but the process of making, then testing, extrapolations can lead to insights. In this case, I imagined that the 2012 enrollment change could continue into the future. Connecting that with the historical record of student numbers increasing immediately created a peak. At the time, I was fascinated by peaks established or forecast in other domains: peak human population, peak car ownership in the American market, peak library book circulation, M. King Hubbert's peak oil forecast, peak beef consumption, and even peak sand. Peak postsecondary enrollment seemed like a potential way of imagining the future.[8]

The idea stayed with me into 2013. I researched, looking into more enrollment data. As was (and remains) my practice, I wrote up peak higher education notes and posted them to my blog, sharing them across social media in order to elicit feedback. Feedback occurred, some supporting the idea, others broadening or challenging it. I published a longer article on the topic in *Inside Higher Ed*, which triggered ripostes from other writers in that journal. I developed a full scenario for workshops and presentations, which I shared with various audiences, from faculty and trustees to government officials. All this feedback shaped the scenario, giving it nuance as well as building my confidence in it. Over the years, I kept tracking down new data to support or dismiss peak, but new enrollment data kept confirming the basic idea. By 2020, the scenario seemed to have substantial descriptive and forecasting powers and so appeared as one scenario among several in *Academia Next*. Audiences no longer expressed surprise when I presented on it, as they increasingly recognized reality bearing it out.[9]

To conclude: *Peak Higher Ed* largely forecasts a challenging and negative time for American higher education, following a similar such decade. Some authors apparently delight in such narratives for various reasons, such as celebrating the apparent decline of an institution they despise for various reasons. I have found many such examples from the political right. There is also a long-running human love for melancholic tales of decline and fall, which seems to appeal to people regardless of their politics. Please do not infer such attitudes for this book or its author. I have devoted most of my life to higher education. I love and celebrate the institution as a powerful force for human flourishing, development, and possibility. The academy has made my life immeasurably richer.

I write here from a position of sadness, seeing the nation's postsecondary sector struggling. I experience that downward trajectory in my work as a professor, facilitator, presenter, consultant, and researcher. As a literature scholar, I considered giving this book the subtitle "A Nightmare," in the spirit of G. K. Chesterton's 1908 novel *The Man Who Was Thursday: A Nightmare*. That narrative depicts a current situation (some contemporary left-wing politics) taken to a higher and more dangerous level, one which stands as a warning to the reader. That the present book is nowhere near that specifically focused on politics is one reason I set the subtitle aside, but the notion of depicting a worsening situation in an admonitory way remains.

Yet those dark spirits and, hopefully, this book are leavened by the belief that academics and their allies can avoid the worst features of the post-peak era and instead seize this moment to redesign a greater academy, one that is even more brilliant and also more humane. We can reimagine and bring to reality colleges and universities that rise rather than fall. I hope this book helps us in some small way to make that shift from being the downslope of a statistical peak and instead move toward a new and different height.

CHAPTER 1

Peak Higher Education, the First Decade

To introduce this scenario, we may say that American higher education passed its peak around the academic years 2011–12. At that point, student enrollment reached a historic high, as did the number of postsecondary institutions. Afterward, enrollment declined gradually, then more sharply during the COVID-19 pandemic, only showing slight growth more than a decade later, in 2023–24. The number of colleges and universities fluctuated and overall declined. A generation of steady institutional growth came to an end, marking an epochal reversal in American higher education.[1]

Those numbers are the evidentiary basis for the peak higher education scenario. The purpose of this chapter is to identify and develop that evidence, exploring the outlines and limitations of the model. We will explain the importance and implications of this data. We will narrate the history and analyze reasons for its occurrence, from anxiety over student debt to shifting popular attitudes toward colleges and universities. How the scenario might develop in its second decade is the subject of the next chapter.

The background of a peak story is, necessarily, the story of a rise. The overall arc of twentieth-century American academia was one of impressive and influential growth. Many people understand this on a qualitative level, recognizing the sector's reputational strength. Various historical events buttress this awareness: the flood of veterans into higher education through the GI Bill, the Sputnik shock and resulting science and technology boom, the massive spread of community colleges across the nation, and various inventions and businesses spun out of academia, from Google to Facebook.

We can back up this sensibility with quantitative history. Federal data shows student numbers soaring over the past century. Just over 2 million people enrolled in colleges and universities during the late 1940s, while *over 21 million* took classes in 2011, a more than tenfold increase. We can trace historical events and eras through this enrollment arc. We might glimpse the reaction to Sputnik as a surge in enrollment through student totals, building from 3.3 million in 1957 to 4.1 million just four years later. The turbulent 1960s saw postsecondary numbers rise from 4.1 to 8.5 million, a doubling encompassing an exceptional period of academic politics and culture. A generation later, under President Bill Clinton, the era emphasized college retraining and accordingly witnessed student numbers grow from 14.4 million in 1992 to 15.3 million in 2000. The twenty-first century, with its STEM boom and focus on knowledge work, took that number to 21 million in just one decade. American higher education entered the new century's second decade with a large and burgeoning population.

We have spoken of total student numbers as the core metric for this scenario, and it is worth pausing to expand on the point. To begin with, teaching is, of course, a critical mission for colleges and universities. While academic institutions perform other missions depending on their constitutions, notably research and service, those are not so widespread throughout the postsecondary sector in terms of campus operations or sheer academic labor. Indeed, teaching is foremost for many institutions, particularly community colleges, as well as state universities and liberal arts colleges not strategically committed to scholarship as a primary focus. Now, considering American higher education as a whole, research appears to be impressive in terms of prizes won, publication counts, and international rankings. We will return to research later in this chapter.

For the moment, we can proceed with a focus on the core mission of teaching.

Second, teaching plays a critical role not only for institutional missions but also for their finances. Most colleges and universities depend heavily on student payments (tuition, primarily; room and board for residential students; and other associated fees) to balance budgets. As Joey King and Brian Mitchell observe pithily, "Enrollment is code for revenue." This is often the case for state colleges and universities, which, despite their public nature, have historically seen government funding decline since the 1970s. This pattern is uneven geographically, with some states offering more generous support than others. State funding also varies by time as governments respond to crises, such as the 2008 Great Recession, as well as to shifts in political priorities and ideologies. Nonetheless, we can observe that, generally speaking, public higher education has increasingly depended on student payments to survive. Private colleges and universities, of course, lack that form of state support.[2]

From this, we can deduce that rising enrollment is good news for a campus's bottom line, and this is often the case. However, the institutional practice of tuition discounting complicates this deduction. In American higher education, relatively few students pay the full, published tuition price. Many students pay less through various discounts, such as grants and work-study. In effect, the full-pay students support or subsidize the rest. Tuition discounting has been increasing over the past decades, rising to more than 50% at some institutions, with even higher rates for first-year students. Therefore, an increase in student numbers does not necessarily mean a powerful income stream, as much depends on what proportion of fees students (or their families) actually pay. Nonetheless, an increase in student numbers offers the possibility of increased institutional revenue, while an enrollment decline will most likely depress income.[3]

The practice of increasing discount rates has an unfortunate side effect in terms of public attitudes. Within the world of higher education finance, the difference between published tuition and fees and the reality of discounts is well known. However, the public is usually not aware of that gap. Instead, what galvanizes attention is rising posted prices, and those can soar to great heights. To pick one extreme example, for several years, I have gathered information about the most expensive campuses with the aim of forecasting when the first one would crack six figures per year in published student prices. In 2024, I identified two dozen colleges and universities, all with excellent reputations and rankings, with prices over $90,000 per year. These numbers may appall (or impress) nonacademics, and perhaps the first one to crest the $100,00 a year barrier will trigger public outcry. In contrast, within academia, chief financial officers and economists understand that only a portion of students and their families will actually pay those amounts. They know that the full-pay or "full freight" population supports the rest, but most other people will simply boggle at the thought of spending nearly half a million dollars for a single Bachelor of Arts degree. Furthermore, academics are aware of the huge diversity of institutional types, knowing that only a slice of these colleges and universities charge truly high amounts, and that many state universities and community colleges are vastly more affordable. We know that some institutions go to great lengths to support students from poor financial backgrounds. Yet media coverage usually downplays that reality in favor of a "tuitions of the rich and famous" style. Perhaps the most prominent example of this in recent years was the Varsity Blues scandal, where wealthy parents spent lavishly to get their offspring into elite institutions. That story even inspired a Lifetime docudrama, the uncreatively named *College Admissions Scandal* (2019).[4]

Further, there is a political or cultural goal involved in increasing enrollment, beyond the sustainability or aspirations of a given college. During the past century, growing student numbers have responded to policy or popular goals: more engineering students to respond to the Soviet threat, for example, and then more computer science graduates as the internet expanded. Another goal emerged over time, that of "college for everyone." This drive was predicated upon a public benefit model of postsecondary education, whereby the economy grows from the work of more college graduates. Public health, civic participation, and other benefits flow from rising numbers of students taking higher education classes. Private benefits also arrive in response to the idea of "the college premium": higher lifetime earnings with a university degree than without. Popular culture, K-12 curricular design, academic and career counseling, and millions of families expressed this view of getting more and more people into college classes. The fact of rising enrollment through 2012 showed students, faculty, and staff had collaborated to fulfill this goal. (We will have more to say on this point in chapter three.)

So, overall enrollment grew through the first decade of the twenty-first century, as noted, and started the second decade following that growth curve. After teaching 20,313,594 students in 2009, 2010 saw campuses enroll a historically high 21,019,438 people, according to federal data. In 2011, that number ticked down slightly, to 21,010,590, which could have been due to statistical noise. After all, 1984 saw a similar downward tick, from 12,464,661 to 12,241,940, yet that was preceded and followed by decades of steady growth. Yet 2012 saw another slight dip, down to 20,644,478, a decrease of roughly 1.8%. In 2013, total enrollment slipped slightly again to 20,376,677, followed by 20,209,092 in 2014. The next year, 2015, showed the total below 20 million, down to 19,988,204. By 2019, the decline reached 19,630,178, or 93% of the peak.

All of this decline occurred *before* the COVID-19 pandemic. The enrollment decline caused by that disaster is better known. National Center for Educational Statistics (NCES) data reports 2020 student numbers as 19,027,410, followed by 18,659,851 in 2021, just under 89% of the 2010 total. *The Hechinger Report* summarizes this as a 15% decline from 2010 to 2021. At this point, the published NCES data ends, and we need to consult other sources.[5]

Before we leave NCES, we should note their undergraduate enrollment data, which follows the same pattern. After twentieth-century growth, the year 2000 shows 13,155,393 undergraduates, a number which builds up to a height of 18,082,427 in 2010. The same gentle decline we saw earlier sets in with our peak moment of 2011, each year slightly shaving numbers off, until we reach 15,397,482 in 2022.[6]

We can find similar evidence from another research enterprise. The National Student Clearinghouse Research Center has been collecting enrollment data through its own methodology, based on surveys of participating institutions. We can track a very similar rising enrollment curve from their publications. Clearinghouse estimates total student numbers in 2010 to be 20,510,526, peaking in 2011 at 20,556,272. Following this peak, a gradual decline set in, with 20,195,924 in 2012 and 19,885,203 in 2013, a 1–2% dip each year, reaching 18,239,874 in 2019. COVID years saw a deeper dip, with 17,778,484 in fall 2020 and 17,302,364 in 2021, standing at 84.1% of peak. Since then, Clearinghouse data continues, unlike that of NCES, and shows an interesting reversal of the trend. Enrollments in 2023 actually rebounded by 1.1% and in 2024 again rose by 0.4%.[7]

We can close this survey of the historical evidence for peak enrollment, its rise and decline, by noting that these numbers appear during a time when the overall United States population rose steadily. Enrollment growth through 2011–12 paralleled the total population growth, in other words. Then, after the peak, the former's decline diverged from the latter's continued growth. To the extent America sought college for everyone, with every year, we fell even further from achieving that goal. In other words, not only did enrollment decline in *absolute* numbers, but it shrank even more sharply *as a proportion* of the nation's population.

While enrollment declined, the number of academic institutions serving that population also slid downward. Federal data shows the total number of all postsecondary enterprises peaking at 7,253 in 2012–13, encompassing every type of institution, including vocational and technical schools. After that, the number dropped every subsequent year: 7,236 (2013–14); 7,151 (2014–15); 7,021 (2015–16); 6,606 (2016–17); 6,502 (2017–18); 6,138 (2018–19); 5,999 (2019–20); and 5,916 (2020–21). The NCES describes this quite starkly: "The number of postsecondary Title IV institutions in 2020–21 was 5,916, compared with 7,021 in 2010–11." This decline occurred across all NCES categories: public institutions (1,981 to 1,892), private nonprofits (1,820 to 1,754), and especially for-profits (3,452 to 2,270). Title IV campuses fell from 4,726 to 3,931, with two-year colleges falling from 1,700 to 1,294 while four-year schools dropped from 3,026 to 2,637. Subsequent years saw this trend continue, with a further 2% decline during the end of President Joe Biden's administration: "Title IV institutions in the U.S. and other jurisdictions decreased from 5,918 in 2022–23 to 5,819 in 2023–24." In short, institutional numbers and enrollment roughly paralleled each other.[8]

Once we examine contemporary higher education through the peak model, we can start to see other signs and potential indicators of decline. The American academic research enterprise has suffered significant wear over the past decade. Scholarly publishing continues to be under financial stress. Monograph sales had already been in decline since the 1980s, reaching a "far lower distribution over the past two decades." The replication crisis has thrown large swaths of published work into question, notably in the social sciences. Allied to this has been a steady flow of stories about researchers found to be cheating or retracting papers due to disabling errors. It is an open question, however, whether those mistakes and unethical acts occurred at a higher level in the 2010s and 2020s than in previous years.[9]

The peak model is by no means universally applicable. We have noted that it applies unevenly, as, for example, the most well-endowed campuses with the highest reputation are immune to decline. Broken down by fields of study, humanities programs are generally seeing drops in enrollment. At least one scholarly book pondered the end of some of those disciplines. In contrast, STEM, business, and allied health have grown. There are political differences across the nation and over time as different state governments pursue varied policies. And some indicators do not clearly show a decline. The total number of workers at Title IV institutions has oscillated rather than clearly dropped, reaching a peak in 2023–24 at 4,029,311, with a significant COVID-era dip, down to 3,868,066, but it does not follow a downward curve overall.[10]

Other dimensions of American academic transformation are harder to determine. Changes in the quality of instruction, for example, are famously or notoriously difficult to quantify. While there are various tests, none have won sufficiently broad acceptance for us to decide whether teaching declined over the past decade. Indeed, perhaps the most famous and controversial negative assessment of teaching quality appeared in 2011 and has yet to be followed by a comparative study. It is easier to point to data about K-12, such as the Programme for International Student Development (PISA) or the National Assessment of Educational Progress (NAEP), or to the very broad assessment of national intelligence known best as the Flynn effect; none of these helps us track postsecondary instruction per se. Related measures, such as grade inflation, are too derivative or unreliable.[11]

Hypotheses for Decline

What caused this falloff from peak American enrollment? We can begin answering this question by considering potential changes in several attitudes, as a kind of demand-side understanding. Popular attitudes toward the nation's higher education ecosystem have begun to slide downward. Repeated surveys show Americans souring on higher education, becoming more skeptical and negative in their views. A 2018 Pew Research study found a solid majority seeing colleges and universities moving in the wrong direction. Younger people and Republicans were more likely than elders and Democrats to express this opinion. Gallup polls offered parallel findings. In 2013, 70% of adults saw higher education as "very important," a number which dwindled to 51% in 2019. Meanwhile, the number of those who deemed academic experience "not too important" more than doubled, rising from 6% to 13% between those two surveys. As with Pew, age differences were clear, with adults closest to traditional college age populations becoming ever more negative:

> The drop has been especially pronounced—33 percentage points—among adults aged 18 to 29. As a result, younger adults are now less likely than middle-aged adults and seniors to consider college as very important, whereas the different age groups held similar perceptions in 2013.[12]

Another Gallup series saw further souring over time. The number of Americans who thought college was affordable and accessible decreased from 2011 to 2019. Younger respondents were more skeptical of academia's availability than other Americans. Still another Gallup poll sequence found worsening confidence in higher education from 2015 to 2024. Criticisms included "colleges pushing political agendas, not teaching relevant skills, and being overly expensive." Republicans became more critical than Democrats. These surveys don't break down how these attitudes might translate into enrollment decisions, but the reader can infer they shaped conversations, advice, and thinking among families, individual would-be students, and advisors, both formal and otherwise.[13]

A second key factor, closely tied to the first, is concern over student debt. American colleges and universities have shifted their payment model over the past generation to one deeply grounded in loans. While some may exaggerate the specter of debt, with media stories of underemployed graduates with huge balances, the reality is indeed daunting. The total amount of student loans stands between $1.6 and $1.8 trillion, as of this writing, a sum extraordinary in American history and also on the world stage. Indeed, we might view the rest of the world's refusal to adopt United States-style massive student debt as a kind of silent judgment on the practice. No other nation has decided to redesign its postsecondary education sector into a gigantic debt generator on this American scale. Parental and student anxiety over debt and price remains high, as polls and conversations show. To be fair, many sources proclaim the pecuniary benefits of a college degree, making that level of debt appear to be a fair investment. A lifetime earnings bonus of hundreds of thousands of dollars is surely a fine outcome for a smaller amount of debt, and this occurs often enough, especially in higher-paying fields as well as when students graduate from campuses with the highest reputations.[14]

However, the outcome is not guaranteed. An HEA Group study found segments of the college graduate population to be earning as much as those with only high school diplomas. A similar proportion made wages just 50% higher than the federal poverty level. These outcomes make the college experience less of a reliable course of action and more of a gamble. Moreover, the median debt burdens of $20,000–$30,000 might pay off over a lifetime, but can look disempowering or horrifying to teenagers or lower-income adults. Worse still is the large number of students who took classes, accrued debt, but failed to win degrees, a position that yields little benefit on the job market. While some might view them as failing in postsecondary education, others might view the system as having failed them—expensively, and with a serious opportunity cost.[15]

The reasons for rocketing student debt are fairly clear. State governments have reduced their support for public institutions since the early 1980s, albeit unevenly in space (between states) and time (fluctuations in response to political demands and financial crises). While public funding has started to recover, it remains below mid-twentieth-century levels. Institutional prices have also grown, for reasons we can grasp. Campus budgets rose in response to rising enrollment (again, before circa 2012), as institutions hired more faculty and staff to handle burgeoning classes. Some colleges and universities increased their standard of student care, which entailed hiring more staff. Regulatory compliance became more extensive, similarly requiring more paid staff. Other costs rose, such as health care, given the unusual complexity and high prices of America's medical system; court rulings have sometimes kept campuses from sharing and thus reducing costs. Information technology funding rose as digital demands soared from the launch of the World Wide Web. Inflation during the early 2020s pushed all kinds of operational costs higher. The end of low interest rates elevated debt financing burdens. The COVID years, of course, saw residential institutions lose room and board revenue, albeit offset to a degree by federal support. These accumulating drivers all pushed college and university costs up, which, absent twentieth-century levels of state funding for public institutions, drove higher prices for students. Debt ballooned in response.[16]

Related to debt is the question of academic credentials for jobs. Many in academia and their supporters view postsecondary attainment as beneficial for the labor market, but that view is not universally held. Professor Neil Krause has argued that federal data shows employers demonstrating a persistent and healthy demand for applicants without college degrees for certain jobs. Further, a significant number of graduates work for a significant number of years in positions requiring little of their postsecondary education, raising the problem of degree-job mismatch. A related critique sees employers demanding too much in the way of university education, a phenomenon driven in part by aggressive credentialism from professional associations and state or local governments. If prospective students entertain these thoughts, perhaps inspired by learning from people with underwhelming degree outcomes, they might consider college a risky bet given such iffy job payoffs and be less likely to apply. Independent researcher Dahn Shaulis has referred to a "college meltdown"; people who perceive the sector in that light would surely be unlikely to participate in it.[17]

Instead, would-be students might pursue alternatives. Boot camps, intensive, short programs offering immersive training experience in a specific skillset, such as computer coding, have for years been competing with colleges. They are by no means perfect, as some providers have oversold their work and others have provided poor learning, and they are definitely not a substitute for an associate's or bachelor's degree, nor do they offer a general education. Their design is aimed squarely at competing with college on specific points: a far shorter experience with far less debt, pointing graduates straight into employment. It is easy to see the attraction given the twenty-first century's postsecondary environment. Alternatively, for some people, heading directly into the labor force for the skilled trades or service sector jobs holds several benefits: a lack of debt, making money straight away without the opportunity cost of years in classrooms.

Along with weakening demand, the first signs of decreasing supply have emerged: a reduction in potential student numbers. We will address the major demographic factors in the next chapter as they will become more salient in the next decade, but for now we can note that what is blandly referred to as the demographic transition (i.e., people having fewer children and living much longer) is starting to appear in parts of the United States. The Northeast and the Midwest, in particular, are seeing that transformation commence, accelerated by internal migration to states in the South and West. In practical terms, this means K-12 enrollment is starting to decline, which yields a shrinking recruitment pool for postsecondary institutions serving traditional-age undergraduates. The reader should recall that the Midwest and especially the Northeastern regions are especially rich in established colleges and universities and are therefore more exposed to demographic risk than other parts of the country.[18]

There have been many attempts to encourage young people to graduate from high school and then advance to colleges and universities, yet their impacts seem muted in the long term, after the peak we describe in this book. Billionaire Michael Bloomberg's effort to increase low-income student enrollment is perhaps the most high-profile failure along these lines, a very expensive initiative that ultimately sent very few students to college. At the same time as these efforts occurred, antithetical initiatives developed. Peter Thiel's famous or notorious program to pay people not to go to college received a great deal of attention, but did not impact many people. Instead, we should think of the national push to get more young people working in trades, as mentioned above. Matthew B. Crawford's thoughtful case for working by hand is relevant here, as is the similar and higher-profile campaign by Michael Rowe. The latter runs the mikeroweWORKS Foundation with the primary goal of nudging students out of the academic path and into working directly in trades. That nonprofit gives millions of dollars in grants each year to make that swerve happen.[19]

We can sum up this survey of the first post-peak decade by observing that enrollment decline in a way that shattered decades of academic history, posing challenges to higher education's sustainability and mission. The reasons for the decline are manifold, stretching across a range of attitudes and perceptions. The question that follows logically is, will this decline continue to play out over the next decade? That is the subject of our next chapter.

CHAPTER 2

Forces Pushing Academia Further Downslope

We have to honestly and aggressively attack the universities in this country.

—AMERICAN VICE PRESIDENT J.D. VANCE

If American higher education reached a peak around the year 2012 and declined over the decade since, how might the academic ecosystem change over the next ten years? In this chapter, we will continue our development of the peak higher education scenario. Having grounded it in a sketch of recent history, we will now extend the model ahead to imagine a persistent post-peak academic world.

The model: as noted earlier, this is one scenario, a single potential future of many. Other scenarios are possible, and multiple futures can play out across the broad and complex landscape of the American postsecondary landscape. Our purpose here is to dive more deeply into this one narrative, extending it forward in time, fleshing out the details, in order to tease out its contours and implications. This will, hopefully, give academics insight into planning and anticipating the next decade of higher education.

What forces might continue to move higher education downslope?[1]

To begin with, the demographic transition mentioned in the previous chapter looks very likely to continue. We can briefly summarize that tremendous and still not seriously appreciated transformation as an effect of modernity. Generally speaking, once a society goes through some form of modernization, from industrialization to postindustrial life, it accumulates wealth, improves health care, and enhances public health. At the same time, the status of women improves, as girls and adult women get more access to the labor market, reproductive autonomy, and especially education, often via some political organization. The combination of those factors massively depresses childbirth rates while extending lifespans. That decline in childbirth descends past a key threshold, roughly 2.1 children born to each adult woman; above this number, a society increases in total population, while below it the number shrinks. This process has been extensively observed for decades on multiple continents, including in the United States.

It seems likely that this demographic transition will continue. Governments that have attempted to encourage women to have more children, from Singapore to Hungary, China, and Denmark, have generally failed. Offers of tax benefits and cash payments, appeals to national spirit, humorous ad campaigns aimed at expanding family life, and religious efforts have proven thus far unable to undo this massive revolution in human reproduction. Put another way, if all American women of childbearing age magically decided to start conceiving children at nineteenth-century levels, and if they were biologically and otherwise practically able to do so, the resulting swarm of offspring would not appear in college classrooms until the year 2044. In reality, the K-12 pipeline is likely to continue narrowing, further reducing the supply of traditional-age would-be undergraduates.

This is a global issue, with multiple countries experiencing and trying to grapple with it. To pick one instance, Japan is a demographic transition leader, seeing primary and secondary school student populations dwindle. A majority of the nation's universities are already seeing enrollment declines. Yet strong national differences are now apparent, as birth rates divide sharply by developmental status. Countries and regions that have processed through modernity, such as Europe, Russia, China, South Korea, and Japan have seen birthrates fall below the 2.1 threshold and drop toward one, while developing nations like Pakistan, Afghanistan, Mongolia, and a group of sub-Saharan nations have birthrates at higher levels. The global average fertility rate fell from nearly 5 in 1950 to 2.23 in 2021. There are many implications for national policies, geopolitics, culture, and more in this massive change in human society. For reasons of space, we will confine our discussion to educational ramifications in the United States.[2]

America is also subject to the demographic transition, but relatively high international immigration rates have masked that to some extent. American birth rates have indeed fallen to historic lows since 2000, reaching 1.66 births per woman, significantly below the 2.1 level, according to the Centers for Disease Control and Prevention (CDC). The CDC recently observed that American childbirth rates were not only "below replacement" but that "the rate has generally been below replacement since 1971 and consistently below replacement since 2007." Yet the nation's population still grows, albeit by small and steady amounts (roughly 0.9% per year), primarily due to international immigration. The United States Census recently reported that "net international migration . . . accounted for the majority of the nation's growth." Politics can, of course, shape immigration through various means, including implementing policies that seek to increase or decrease incoming numbers, as well as changing the sending nations and regions. As this book was composed, larger numbers flowed into the United States for several years, under the Biden presidency, followed by a major reduction under the second Trump administration. We may see immigration depressed for at least several years, depending on national political decisions and global perception of them. This will, to some extent, accelerate the American demographic transition.[3]

It is possible that fertility rates will fall even further for not just cultural but also biological reasons. Human sperm count in several nations, including the United States, has declined for decades according to research and meta-analysis, although such research remains contested. Recent work assessing the impact of hundreds of endocrine disruptors—a series of environmental items, including microplastics and "forever chemicals"—has found initial signs of a depressed effect on human reproductive capacity. Lifestyle issues also play a role in depressed fertility, including the age of would-be parents. In other words, should we decide culturally to return to older, elevated childbirth, we would still contend with biological drivers pushing us toward lower levels.[4]

Some readers will be familiar with the phrase "demographic cliff," and that term actually describes a different and much more limited phenomenon. Carleton College economist Nathan Grawe memorably coined the phrase to describe a singular event. During the financial crash of 2008, sometimes dubbed the Great Recession, many women decided not to have children in response to the crisis and its many economic uncertainties. That sharp downturn in infants then progressed through K-12 grades in the form of smaller class sizes until it is now about to start appearing in postsecondary admissions. The demographic cliff is a powerful feature amid the broader landscape of declining fertility within the demographic transition.[5]

It is important to recall that demographics are not necessarily destiny, as the saying goes. Our choices matter a great deal in shaping what happens to the people who are actually born and live their lives. We could collectively act to boost higher education graduation rates, for example, to better prepare those students for college study, and to encourage more adults to take classes. There are optimistic views along those lines. The latest Western Interstate Commission for Higher Education forecast estimated the number of high school graduates to decline from 3.9 to 3.4 million by 2041: a significant decline, but not a shattering one. Yet changing demographics condition our choices by reshaping the options we have. For the purposes of this peak higher education scenario, we will presume the demographic transition continues, sharpened by Grawe's cliff, and impacting academic enrollment.[6]

A second factor that might continue the peak higher education story is that of stressed institutional finances. Here we are not referring to the wealthiest institutions, which enjoy a disproportionate share of media coverage and the academic discourse, but to the majority of colleges and universities, which lack substantial financial resources and depend on student fees to keep operating. Enrollment declines can cut revenue, as we discussed earlier. Further, increasing tuition discounts may entice more students to apply and even attend, but can reduce net revenue overall.

Recall that the practice of steep tuition discounts can allow published tuition and fees to rise. In the previous chapter, we noted colleges and universities posting annual prices over $90,000. At some point in the next decade, we should see those campuses, then others, break through the six-figure barrier and charge more than $100,000 per year. Depending on media coverage, that news might elicit criticism and outright horror, not to mention calls for public and private action. Passing the six-figure per annum milestone might depress interest in academia to a degree.[7]

As noted in the previous chapter, a series of economic pressures exert themselves on academic institutions. Operating costs continue to rise, driving up tuition, which in turn can depress enrollment. Early 2020s inflation exacerbated this problem, spiking up certain costs. According to one account, "A recent budget proposal by University of Minnesota's interim president included some form of the word 'inflation' 25 times, citing increased costs for food, services and labor, among other things."[8] Heightened inflation persists, as of this writing, although the Trump administration vows to reduce it. Deferred maintenance for the campus-built environment leads to higher costs down the road, along with experiential problems with damaged or degraded buildings. Rising institutional costs overall seem unlikely to change, absent a benevolent revolution in American health care financing and similar revolutions in maintenance costs, not to mention less benevolent changes to faculty and staff compensation.

The national and global picture is vital in this context. Indeed, a low national unemployment rate may drive up salaries and benefits, which is fine news for those workers but adds to an institution's balance sheet. Climate disasters and threats will drive up insurance costs, both in terms of rising payments and decreasing payouts (we will see more on this in chapter five). Constant cyberattacks will increase IT costs on multiple levels: hiring and retaining more cybersecurity staff; training and retraining an institution's entire population on safety protocols; licensing more defensive software; and paying ransom or for infrastructure and data recovery. Cyber threats may escalate as the global geopolitical situation becomes more unstable and dangerous, especially to the extent that the United States is directly involved. Rising federal and state financial support appears unlikely to return to generous levels, especially under a wildly cutting second Trump administration. That same government could well spur additional financial challenges in the short and medium term, such as by cutting federal financial support or conducting trade wars, which have negative consequences for colleges and universities. Slowing economic growth globally could also impact American campuses, despite that nation's relative strength, depending on investment exposure and international operations, such as overseas branch campuses and global student recruitment.

Publicly available assessments of these financial problems exist, although they rarely receive much open discussion. A leading accounting firm, Ernst and Young, assessed *nearly one-half* of four-year institutions as either being at risk or requiring close monitoring. S&P Global Ratings (formerly Standard & Poor's) found roughly one-third of colleges and universities, especially private ones, to have lower credit standings, including some so risky as to be deemed "speculative." They found that the group is likely to "continue to expand as more institutions have been increasingly strained by enrollment and operating pressures." On the governmental side, the United States Department of Education regularly publishes (or published, depending on the second Trump administration) a list of colleges and universities it identifies as being at some level of financial risk or in need of "Heightened Cash Monitoring." The indicators used express various signs of trouble. "Schools may be placed on HCM1 or HCM2 as a result of compliance issues including but not limited to accreditation issues, late or missing annual financial statements and/or audits, outstanding liabilities, denial of re-certifications, concern around the school's administrative capabilities, concern around a school's financial responsibility, and possibly severe findings uncovered during a program review."[9]

The most recent report available, December 1, 2024, lists more than 460 institutions. They range from for-profit professional schools to community colleges and state universities, from Paul Quinn College and the Florida Academy of Nursing to the Dominican University of California and Michigan State University.[10]

There is also a vicious cycle to such information becoming public. News of a college's financial problems can depress applications as students fear studying at a campus that might cut its services or cease to exist. Similarly, such accounts can block donations. Some donors would contribute to keep a beloved institution afloat, as we have seen in some cases, such as Sweet Briar College. Yet other would-be givers might hesitate to support an institution that seems to mishandle funds, provide a declining experience for students, or might go dark.

A third driver for post-peak academia would be continued negative attitudes among would-be students and the American population as a whole. In the previous chapter, we saw how popular perceptions of higher education had soured during the past decade. Should that negativity persist or strengthen, enrollment, government support, and philanthropy may well decline. A 2024 Pew survey is instructive here. That poll found 40% of Americans do not view higher education as valuable, viewing it as "not too or not at all important." Other signs of skepticism or dismissal include:

- Roughly half (49%) say it's less important to have a four-year college degree today in order to get a well-paying job than it was 20 years ago; 32% say it's more important, and 17% say it's about as important as it was 20 years ago.
- Only 22% say the cost of getting a four-year college degree today is worth it even if someone has to take out loans. Some 47% say the cost is worth it only if someone doesn't have to take out loans. And 29% say the cost is not worth it.

A further Pew survey found Americans increasingly unhappy with science in particular. While a slim majority think "science has had a mostly positive effect on society," that number had stepped down since 2021 and 2019. One-third of Americans think science has equally positive and negative effects. The bitter COVID-19 controversies over public health clearly played a role in this reduction in support. Worse, "roughly a quarter of Americans (27%) now say they have not too much or no confidence in scientists to act in the public's best interests, up from 12% in April 2020." Once more, Republicans are more negative in their attitudes than Democrats. We perhaps see an expression of this in the second Trump administration's decisions to cut a great deal of federal scientific research support. While not all academics are scientists (a majority are not) and not all scientists are academics (others work for businesses, nonprofits, and governments), the implication is that this negative attitude applies to academia to some degree. To the extent that Americans consider academic science to be more a matter of research than teaching, this negative view will tend to apply more to research universities than the rest of the sector. If we view science as something that higher education does across the board, from research to teaching and service, then the whole college and university world is involved.[11]

A 2024 Foundation for Individual Rights and Expression (FIRE)/National Opinion Research Center, University of Chicago (NORC) survey found similar divergences of opinion with rising negativity over time. In their findings, "fewer Americans reported 'a great deal' or 'quite a lot' of confidence in colleges and universities . . . and more Americans reported 'very little' confidence or 'none at all.'" Partisan differences continue to be apparent, as in both FIRE/NORC and Pew surveys, Republicans were more critical than independents and especially of Democrats. Yet other groups show negativity as well:

> Some of the largest drops in confidence in higher education are within subgroups: among Americans ages 18–34, Democrats, and women. . . . As such, the current dip in confidence in colleges and universities is largely driven by groups that previously had quite a lot of confidence in higher education. Americans

ages 18–34 with "a great deal" or "quite a lot" of confidence dropped from 42% to 22% since last summer. For Democrats the drop was from 59% to 42%, and for women, from 39% to 29%. These groups appear to be playing catch-up in ways that do not bode well for colleges and universities.[12]

FIRE/NORC also found views declining after the Gaza protests. This suggests the possibility that further visible signs of global geopolitical stress within academia may further repress the sector's reputation. We could think of student (and staff and faculty) protests over multiple incidents and events, as well as actions taken over international policies involving curricula, foreign investments, and faculty/staff from other nations. Any of these could become flashpoints for anti-academic animus, especially if accelerated by political activists. Student activism often fascinates journalists who report on it extensively, especially in the rare instances involving property destruction, personal violence, and confrontation with police.[13]

Such political activism has grown to become a major target and theme of the Trump era Republican Party. The 2017–2021 administration often criticized academia, but also financially supported it, notably through the 2020 Coronavirus Aid, Relief, and Economic Security Act (CARES) Act. Out of power, Trump targeted colleges and universities more energetically, slamming academics as extremists, Marxists, lunatics, and more. His campaign for a return to office continued this theme. His vice-presidential candidate, J.D. Vance, followed suit. Before the campaign, Vance urged a national audience to "honestly and aggressively attack the universities in this country." In that speech, he stated that "our universities transmit not knowledge and not truth but deceit and lies." Vance also quoted Richard Nixon, charging that "the professors are the enemy."[14]

Supporting this attitude was the Heritage Foundation's influential Project 2025, including the *Mandate for Leadership* book, which described a multipronged campaign against postsecondary education. This called for shutting down or breaking up the federal Department of Education, prosecuting librarians for giving access to pornography, "reinstituting the National Security Higher Education Advisory Board," ending student loan forgiveness, privatizing student loans, ending the National Education Association's federal charter, undoing the Biden administration's Title IX regulations, cutting reimbursement for universities' indirect research costs, and ending teaching of and research into DEI, gender fluidity, and climate change. Project 2025 also called for setting up new, national-security-focused academies while reducing academic requirements for federal jobs.[15]

Following the 2024 election and 2025 inauguration, the second Trump administration followed up on these ideas. As of this writing it has cut billions of dollars in federal funding to research universities; attempted to end the Department of Education; seized and attempted to deport thousands of international students; ended federal support for DEI, gender, and climate research and teaching; terminated programs like the Institute of Museum and Library Services (IMLS) and the Education Resources Information Center (ERIC); launched investigations into dozens of colleges and universities for alleged antisemitism; successfully coerced Columbia University to change internal procedures and place an academic department under receivership; and cut funding for campus decarbonization. The Trump administration's actions have inspired multiple states to take legislative action against their colleges and universities, from Ohio to Kentucky. In response, Moody's Ratings downgraded its outlook for all of higher education to negative. It is unclear how many other actions the government may take against academia. It is also uncertain how many of these actions will be reversed. But they indicate significant pressures on higher education, likely to drive it further downslope from peak, not to mention causing extensive damage to the education and careers of many people.[16]

It is also unclear how the Trump administration's actions will impact public attitudes toward academia. Americans might become more supportive in reaction, feeling sympathy for a wounded sector or that the attacks were unjust. Alternatively, a good number might view Trump's actions as expressions of their own negative attitudes. A weakened college system might appear less attractive to would-be students.

On a personal level, people might rethink the path to and through higher education because they prefer to just get a job instead, as we noted in the previous chapter. If colleges and universities look problematic because of the specter of debt and concerns about academic work paying off in the workforce, then postsecondary education's reputation sinking might further encourage people to avoid taking classes. Allied to this is the increasing perception that college degrees are primarily about getting a well- or better-paying job. We can find many accounts of this shift, some celebratory, some critical. For example, a recent Chronicle of Higher Education article explored the shift in midwestern states. Eric Kelderman reports a conversation with an Iowa guidance counselor:

> In the past, "students were more willing to see college as a way to explore their options and take courses that would guide them on that path," [Maria Sulentic, a counselor for the West Bend-Mallard Consolidated School District] said. "Now they're seeing it as something to do when they know what they want to do and what their end goal is."
>
> If they don't see a clear outcome from college that includes a job, Sulentic said, students are going to consider other options, like working on the family farm or at local businesses.[17]

To the extent this attitude proliferates over the next decade, it will shape applications and student approaches to university work. Consider people—high school students and adults alike—who view a campus's offerings. How will they perceive the parts that do not seem to bear on job prospects? What will they think of the general education curriculum? To what extent will they value learning to learn, discovering their voices, determining their callings, becoming better civic participants, finding partners, seeking mental health, and being entertained by athletics?

Furthermore, as students progress through postsecondary study, increasing numbers feel that their scholarship did not prepare them for the job market. Surveys from *Inside Higher Ed* and the career development company Handshake found that current students express greater anxiety about employment than their predecessors did. Despite low unemployment rates, many feared competitive hiring situations, as well as concerns over being able to pay off their student loans. Handshake found students more satisfied with their personal than professional growth during college. How do such attitudes influence younger people or other adults when they consider applying to university? How will that mindset shape a current student's drive to complete their degree, or to lead them out of the academy and directly into the job market?[18]

A classic rejoinder to such views is that higher education tends to pay off handsomely. There is a "college premium," the addition to their lifetime earnings if they receive college degrees. The argument holds that going to college or university will boost income even with debt and the opportunity cost of years of study. Over a person's postgraduation decades of work, higher compensation will accrue, significantly exceeding one's academic investment. Historically, this has often been the case, although not universally, being complicated by other factors, such as the reputation of a college or university, the reputation of its programs related to a specific job, the identity of a given major, and, of course, an individual's career and life choices.

However, the college premium has lost some of its appeal due to the spread of the aforementioned attitudes. It also appears to have declined in recent years, according to some recent research. One Federal Reserve analysis found the premium declining after a mid-2010s peak, due largely to high school graduates' salaries rising as well as some loss to college graduates. Some underrepresented minorities and poor people saw the most gains in this domain. The authors conclude that "our findings suggest that historically tight labor markets in recent years have changed relative wages, possibly altering the perceived benefits of a college education." David Autor, Arindrajit Dube, and Annie McGrew found something similar: "Rapid relative wage growth at the bottom of the distribution reduced the college wage premium and counteracted around one-third of the four-decade increase in aggregate 90/10 log wage inequality." Another Federal Reserve bank produced a study of the college wealth (as opposed to income) premium, and found that aggregate number declining even more steeply: "Among families whose head is White and born in the 1980s, the college wealth premium of a terminal four-year bachelor's degree is at a historic low; among families whose head is any other race and ethnicity born in that decade, the premium is statistically indistinguishable from zero." A study from the HEA Group and Student Defense found that *one-third* of graduate degrees did not yield economic benefits for their holders. Popular awareness of such data will hardly boost college applications or the public's appreciation of higher education.[19]

Skepticism of higher education now had a clearly gendered dimension. Since the colonial era, men outnumbered women in higher education, but the genders reached parity in the 1980s, and then women became the majority and have been since. In 2021, 6,573,414 males enrolled compared to 8,824,068 females. Now, women are significantly more likely than men to enroll in college after high school, to graduate from there, and to do so more quickly. Celeste Davis and Richard Reeves argue that this might have become a self-reinforcing loop, where boys and men see an environment where girls and women predominate and gradually turn away, making the environment more solidly female and so less appealing to males. We can already find evidence of this in "manosphere" advice for boys and men to avoid an emasculating academic life. Sexism can increasingly drive negative attitudes toward a postsecondary sector more liberally populated by women.[20]

Another troubling shaper of academic attitudes for the next decade comes from the recent COVID-19 experience. Among that disaster's many impacts was widespread learning loss in K-12 students, due to a variety of reasons (teachers having difficulty teaching online for the first time, the experience of a national trauma, sudden economic dislocation). Those traditional-age students have already started appearing in colleges and universities, bringing with them additional needs for some remedial academics as well as a call for socialization. COVID might also depress those numbers, given unusually high rates of pandemic-era and post-pandemic absenteeism. Students who attend college might struggle more than their predecessors. Additionally, if they had a poor educational experience in middle and high schools, they might have a difficult time with the postsecondary version, a problem that could appear as extended time to degree or lower completion rates. Even as the major COVID-19 onslaught recedes, its impacts linger.

Academic research played a key role in addressing that pandemic, but the enterprise has challenges ahead for the next decade. We noted some in the previous chapter, notably the replication crisis, depressed monograph sales, and an outbreak of ethical problems in both research and scholarly communication. As of this writing, academics grapple with each of those challenges, yet all persist. The combination is negative for academic research and its reputation. Further research challenges loom. Some researchers argue that despite a historical rise in the number of scholars over the past generation, their productivity is slowing down, especially in terms of the flow of novel ideas. Scholarly citation skews very low in some fields, notably the humanities, where more than 80% of papers apparently remain uncited over time; some may view this as a problem of overproduction, especially given institutional investments, incentives, and support for such publication.[21]

At a broader level, higher education may also have to cope with competition. We have previously noted some alternatives to higher education, such as boot camps, which have not so far developed into a major challenge at scale, but we should not assume no others will occur. The service economy and skilled trades can attract people seeking careers without debt, as discussed in chapter one. As workers in those fields age up the industries may appeal more strongly to younger workers. On a related point, political economists and policymakers have for decades hoped to create an apprenticeship system akin to those in Switzerland and Germany. To set up such an ecosystem would require major and coordinated action from American industries, K-12 schools, and policymakers. While that has not yet appeared, we should not rule it out, especially as higher education's reputation sours and national politics stand against the sector.

At a still larger level we might expect a different kind of political action against higher education, that of potential downsides from our successes. What are the problems attending on producing ever more graduates? Overproduction of PhDs is a well-known reason for the immense boom in adjuncts within the professoriate, who now constitute the largest proportion of that population. That overproduction is also a driver behind the push to find alternative careers for graduate students beyond becoming faculty members, nicknamed the "alt ac" path.[22]

Moving forward, there may be further results to our long enrollment boom. Peter Turchin has referred to the historical problem of "elite overproduction," identifying examples from history where a nation's elite in various senses (clergy, lawyers, bureaucrats, aristocracy) grew to a point where competition for advancement overheated, building into political crises, such as unrest, civil strife, and revolutions. Turchin and others argue that the long period of growth in American postsecondary enrollment, which we've discussed, may well yield such political chaos as graduates fail to find positions they consider appropriate, and thus turn on each other, or become politically entrepreneurial. If the latter sounds strange, it has ample precedent. As economist Noah Smith observes, stating somewhat tongue-in-cheek,

> A handful of angry, downwardly mobile English Ph.D.s aren't by themselves enough to overthrow the institutions of society, but they can make hugely outsized contributions to unrest and discord if they are so inclined. Remember, these are very smart people who are very good at writing things, and well-schooled in any number of dissident ideas. Those are the kind of people who tend to lead revolutions.[23]

Looking ahead over the next ten or more years, we might see well-credentialed graduates playing such roles. This might in turn elicit backlash, which could build on the increasingly negative reputation higher education is attaining, as critics charge colleges and universities with authoring political chaos—not for the first time.

To return to our theme, after a decade of the post-peak situation, higher education could potentially continue down that negative path. The forces that created the new environment may continue to exercise their influence. Additionally, the deepening demographic transition appears likely to constrain the flow of traditional-age would-be students to colleges and universities, accentuated by Grawe's demographic cliff. Institutional finances remain problematic for a significant number of campuses, which should have a variety of effects on these institutions. Academia's sinking reputation could yield additional or worsened problems, from reductions in state and private funding to further enrollment decline. Such a decline arriving after decades of successful graduate production may also lead to unrest at various political levels.

There is one further dimension to our peak higher education scenario that we have not sufficiently addressed. The long enrollment and institutional growth era was made possible by, and then supported the extension of, pro-academic attitudes. The United States shifted its model of postsecondary education's size and social role. The mid-twentieth century saw a change from college being a "nice to have" for certain elites to becoming a social good, especially for STEM and for serving a post–World War II baby boom. By the end of that century, the social good became increasingly mandatory. "College for all" became accepted as good policy and popular wisdom as we surged the population toward and through academic careers to the best of our collective abilities. Yet after the peak, it seems that the policy and wisdom are starting to fray, even disintegrate. Perhaps the deepest impact of peak higher education is the end of college for everyone. Exploring that possibility is the subject of our next chapter.

CHAPTER 3

After the Consensus Shattered

[Presidential candidate Kamala Harris] told the crowd in the former mining town of Wilkes-Barre, Penn., that "for far too long," the U.S. has "encouraged only one path to success: four-year college."

"Our nation needs to recognize the value of other paths," Harris said, noting the importance of apprenticeships and trade programs.

College for everyone: Many readers will recognize this slogan or the sentiment it describes. For the past generation, America has been effectively united in the desire to expand access to higher education. K-12 schools transformed their curriculum to better prepare ultimate graduates for postsecondary academics. Families, guidance counselors, politicians, and popular culture celebrated the idea that the more people who get more college and university experience, the better it would be for everyone.

The onset of peak higher education threatens to break up this national belief and its supporting practices. Changing attitudes toward academia, as noted in previous chapters, point to its decline. The long enrollment decline suggests that a growing number of potential students are voting with their feet by not walking the "college for all" path.

I have referred to this development as a shattered consensus, and that breakup is the subject of this chapter. We will trace how it came to be, driven by which forces, and having certain effects through a short history of the idea and its practice. Next, we will extend it into the future to see how the idea's decline shapes the post-peak postsecondary world. The breakup of college for everyone is one major dimension of peak higher education.

We can begin understanding the rise of college for all by quickly recapitulating the history of American higher education. It famously began with the founding of Harvard College in 1636, followed by the gradual spread of campuses across the then-British colonies. These institutions primarily educated students for careers in law, government, and the clergy. The colleges and universities taught only a small number of white men, usually of financial means. The first century after the founding of an independent republic saw these institutions grow in number as the country's population did, expanding their missions but remaining small in teaching footprint, focused largely on the social elite.

A single act of congressional legislation in 1862 broke this picture and ignited a major expansion of popular access to postsecondary education. In the midst of the Civil War, Vermont senator Justin Morrill shepherded his "Act Donating Public Lands to the Several States and Territories which May Provide Colleges for the Benefit of Agriculture and the Mechanic Arts" bill, subsequently better known as the Morrill Act, into law. With this, the nation committed to establishing public, state-funded institutions aimed at benefiting the public, massively expanding capacity. Its very name demonstrated its democratic focus on non-elite occupations. The hitherto exclusive nature of American higher education remained in the form of some colleges and universities, many of which retain that identity through the present day. These land grant institutions were not entirely democratic in their foundation, however. Not only did they exclude certain populations from attending and teaching there, but their titular lands were seized from Native American nations.[1]

Afterward, the later nineteenth century saw new forms of institutions, some of which expanded academic access. Small liberal arts colleges, those particularly American inventions, appeared and taught a variety of students. Colleges for women appeared, offering a new way for one-half of the population to study and teach. What we now know as historically Black colleges and universities (HBCUs) appeared after the Civil War, opening higher education to that population. Johns Hopkins University launched a wave of research universities, inspired by German models. Professional schools flourished at both undergraduate and graduate levels, including for-profit ones. A number of junior colleges, the ancestors of today's community colleges, provided low-cost education. Normal schools appeared, intended to prepare students to become K-12 teachers. Some of these opened the way for underrepresented (often white, male) students to attend, especially through a focus on career preparation and practical skills. The number of campuses nearly doubled, from 563 in 1869–70 to 977 in 1899–1900.[2]

That was the era we might characterize as "college for some," even as the number of "some" grew. Then, the twentieth century is where we find the birth of college for all. The inherited nineteenth-century innovations became institutionalized and helped higher education steadily grow. The high school movement encouraged more students to complete more K-12 classes, which generated both more graduates as well as a demand for additional teachers. The Great Depression and World War II suspended this upward arc by draining finances and sending would-be students away from campuses. Yet in 1944, Congress, embarrassed by its failures to support World War I veterans, passed the GI Bill, which provided tuition and living expenses to returning soldiers. This massively expanded enrollment, due to the enormous scale of wartime mobilization, although relatively few women had served and benefited, and the application of the law often discriminated against Black veterans. The emergent Cold War spurred more demand for STEM professionals and scholars. Laws like the federal National Science Foundation Act (1950) and the National Defense Education Act (1958) directed funds to improve science education from primary through postsecondary schools, in addition to research.[3]

Two decades after the GI Bill and in the midst of the rising baby boom, President Lyndon B. Johnson further expanded access to colleges and universities through the Great Society's Higher Education Act (1965). This committed the federal government (as opposed to the states, which operated their public universities) to offering student loans and grants, including establishing Pell Grants, as well as work-study programs, along with some financial support for institutions. It created a National Teachers Corps, which led more students into K-12 faculty careers. Its ambitions were high: to support and encourage any "high school senior anywhere in this great land of ours [to] apply to any college or any university in any of the 50 States and not be turned away because his family is poor." For several decades, subsequent iterations of the HEA further expanded this ambition.[4]

Other developments in the second half of the twentieth century extended Johnson's goal. The 1964 Civil Rights Act worked against racial discrimination in many ways, including in education. The state of California organized its "California Plan" (technically the Donahoe Higher Education Act) in 1960, arranging a three-tiered system of University of California, California State Universities (CSUs), and community colleges; the latter were designed to be free to attend, while CSUs were to be very affordable. Title IX, passed in 1972, banned sex-based discrimination in education, encouraging more girls and women to attend. Other states sought to expand postsecondary access by providing more financial aid, such as Georgia's Helping Outstanding Pupils Educationally (HOPE) program, codified in 1993. President Clinton then used the HOPE name to offer tax credits for students and families. Throughout the nation, community colleges grew extensively in number and in the number of students they taught. The total number of students soared from 7,368,644 in 1970 to 13,155,393 in 2000, nearly doubling. In parallel, the number of institutions did double, from 2,004 in 1960 to 4,084 in 2000. We can see now what motivated Philip G. Altbach to observe in 2016 that "Without question, massification has been the dominating force in higher education in the past half-century or more."[5]

The twenty-first century continued to expand access through various means. Distance learning, which had been a marginal feature of the landscape in the form of correspondence courses and televised lectures, took off with the growth of online classes and degrees as the internet became more accessible, especially through the World Wide Web. The No Child Left Behind law (2001) sought to encourage more postsecondary enrollment by improving the K-12 experience. Its Mathematics and Science Partnerships section funded improvements in STEM teaching. A drive to have state governments support some or all student tuition had some successes, notably the Tennessee Promise (2014). This "last mile" system, which funded community college access, increased enrollment by 40%, including significant gains for Black and Hispanic students. Several national efforts appeared, championed by another Vermont senator, Bernie Sanders, as well as Washington state Representative Pramila Jayapal and presidents Barack Obama and Joe Biden; however, these did not become law. There have been progressive and left-wing calls for expanding access by taxing the wealthy, or financial transactions, or even rich campus endowments.[6]

We might recall Obama's call in his first (2009) State of the Union address, which began with a plea for total participation in education: "It is our responsibility as lawmakers and educators to make this system [of education] work. But it is the responsibility of every citizen to participate in it." The following was this formulation of college for all as a national goal:

> And so tonight, I ask every American to commit to at least one year or more of higher education or career training. This can be community college or a four-year school; vocational training or an apprenticeship. But whatever the training may be, every American will need to get more than a high school diploma. And dropping out of high school is no longer an option. It's not just quitting on yourself, it's quitting on your country—and this country needs and values the talents of every American. That is why we will provide the support necessary for you to complete college and meet a new goal: by 2020, America will once again have the highest proportion of college graduates in the world.[7]

"Every American will need to get more than a high school diploma"—this might be unsurpassed as a call for college for all. And to an extent, the nation heeded President Obama. We noted in a previous chapter that the number of students crested over 18 million in 2011 and the number of campuses at 4,495 in 2009–10. Put another way, the proportion of Americans with four or more years of college rose immensely, from 5.9% in 1940 to 39.6% in 2022.[8]

We can pause our brief historical survey to sketch the rationale behind college for all. There is an overarching idea of public good, that a better educated citizenry is an improvement over one that isn't on numerous metrics: lifetime earnings, physical health, and civic participation. There are narrower public purposes, such as the long-running push for more STEM graduates or the idea that a knowledge-based economy requires workers with more education. One exemplary document described "College for All" as "A necessary investment in our future." Complementing this is the personal, private argument, starting with improved economic outcomes for each graduate but adding to it non-pecuniary benefits: discovering one's passion and voice, exploring the world of ideas, and leading a richer life. Donald Harward describes this as "a 'triad' of interrelated core purposes for liberal education":

> the *epistemic* (coming to know, discovery, and the advancing of knowledge and understanding); the *eudemonic* (the fuller realization of the learner, the actualizing of the person's potential—classically to achieve individual well-being and happiness); and the *civic* (the understanding that learning puts the learner in relation to what is other, to community and its diversity in the broadest sense, as well as the responsibility that comes from sustaining the community and the civic qualities that make both open inquiry and self-realization possible).[9]

We could see that as a nearly utopian longing for mass human improvement. Alternatively, this tri-fold call for more higher education suits multiple needs: economic, civic, moral. There is also a parallel to the high school degree in seeing a college diploma as something every citizen or resident has a right to.

At the same time, we can identify a negative reason for everyone to get some college experience. In her first book, *Lower Ed: The Troubling Rise of*

For-Profit Colleges in the New Economy, Tressie McMillan Cottom explores that underdiscussed sector within higher education and seeks to understand its appeal and persistence. Her conclusion applies to all of higher education, describing our increased demand for it as a response to a neoliberal political economy that privatizes many functions we once expected from the state. An increasingly competitive world of work and a sense that the social safety net is weakening lead us to academics as a way to build individual strength. One aims for one or two degrees beyond high school in order to make more money to pay for more expensive health care, for example, or to boost one's chances of a decent retirement. "Our political choices constructed Lower Ed [for-profit higher education] as a legitimate way to navigate the vicissitudes of the labor market." Further, "When we offer more credentials in lieu of a stronger social contract, it is Lower Ed. When we ask for social insurance and get workforce training, it is Lower Ed. When we ask for justice and get 'opportunity,' it is Lower Ed."[10]

Higher education is what America offers instead of stronger public programs, in other words. "College for all" is an alternative to a stronger social safety net or even Nordic-style democratic socialism. A similar argument comes from another faculty member, viewing expanded college attainment as an academic way to paper over nonacademic (economic) problems:

> Diane Ravitch, the prominent education historian and professor at New York University [argued that] the highest share of college graduates in the world doesn't equal a healthy economy. . . . "We are chasing a fantasy." Our economic and social problems stem more from the wide gap between rich and poor, and jobs sent overseas, says Ms. Ravitch, than from too few people pursuing a bachelor's degree. We're projecting economic insufficiencies onto the education system, she says. "The college-for-all talk is like fairy dust sprinkled over the conversation."[11]

Again, we can extend that view to all of higher education, including its private and public sectors. In that light, community colleges, HBCUs, research-1 universities, liberal arts colleges, military academies, and all are a gigantic attempt at social engineering, reforming society through campuses.

Given these desires and the many ways American society has created to satisfy them, why did college for everyone fall apart? We can begin our answer by recalling our discussion of reasons for peak in chapters one and two, starting with the negative transformation of American public views of colleges and universities. Obviously, a growing number of people who view academia with skepticism or hostility are less likely to support sending more people to its classes. We have cited surveys as evidence, and can add another. A 2023 *Wall Street Journal*/NORC poll found just over one-half of the nation turned against higher education: "56% of Americans think earning a four-year degree is a bad bet." This isn't simply a case of people without postsecondary experience opposing those who do have it: "42% of people *with* college degrees said in the most recent survey that it wasn't worth it, up more than 10 percentage points from the two polls last decade" (emphasis added).[12]

We can return to the party politics dimension of that attitude, which can actively oppose college for all. Republicans are more critical of higher education than either independents or Democrats, as we have noted. For one useful example, Virginia Foxx, a North Carolina Republican in the House of Representatives, refers to the idea as "a harmful myth." She argued that it was foolish to believe only four-year colleges offered the experience necessary to succeed in the labor market, citing historical and current models of successful dropouts, such as Andrew Carnegie and Steve Jobs. Foxx continues her critique by calling out an "over-credentialization craze" which ultimately devalues a college degree. Moreover, she criticizes academic institutions as "unaligned with the needs of employers in their job markets." Other conservative criticisms include seeing academia as producing useless degrees and indoctrinating young people into various left ideologies. Additionally, others castigate academics and graduates as elitists, snobbish and disdainful toward the rest of the population, describing a populist position.[13]

That point about America undervaluing nonacademic knowledge has become a bipartisan idea. Some refer to the "paper ceiling," akin to the glass ceiling preventing women from rising into positions of greater authority and compensation. Here, the lack of a paper (academic credential) blocks worthy individuals from similar ascensions. Higher education already has one set of ways to address this problem through forms of credit for prior learning, which use assessments to create academic recognition of independent study, often through work and life experience. Yet there have been calls to go further than that by moving in the opposite direction, of not increasing ways for people to credential their nonacademic work but by reducing academic expectations and requirements.

Examples of state-level responses to this idea have been appearing in increasing numbers. In 2022, the Republican governor of Maryland removed degree requirements for many state jobs. The next year saw Pennsylvania's Democratic governor do the same, with his official statement emphasizing its cross-party appeal: "Governor Shapiro's executive order action has garnered bipartisan support here in Pennsylvania, with Republicans and Democrats lauding this action." In 2024, the Democratic governor of Massachusetts issued an executive order ending bachelor and associate degree requirements for many of that state's positions. In his account of that event, Nathan Greenfield reminds us that Massachusetts is "the state with the highest per capita number of colleges and universities." At least one dozen states and at least one city, Philadelphia, have since done the same.[14]

Note that in the bipartisan world of reducing degree requirements, some anti-paper-ceiling efforts have been openly progressive. For example, one Democrat-led city's policies directly remove higher education requirements in order to pursue antiracist ends:

> [Mayor] Parker says her goal is to ensure the city's workforce reflects the people of Philadelphia. . . . Parker wants to see more Philadelphia natives and more Black and brown families benefit from careers with the city, which she hopes can be a path to the middle class.
>
> "She believes strongly that there's a lot of people out there that their lived life experience matters and can enable them to do jobs, not just competently, but more than competently," Parker spokesperson Joe Grace said. "She sees these kind of job opportunities as pathways to lift people up." For Parker, that

means removing impediments to advancement for people from diverse backgrounds. While 48% of white Philadelphians have bachelor's degrees, only 18% of Black residents do, making them ineligible to apply for many city jobs.[15]

Some Democratic politicians may also want to support working-class people without degrees because they are concerned about losing touch with that population, as journalist Rachel Cohen considered. "After decades of prioritizing college attendance, the Democratic Party has been scrambling to figure out how to change the widespread perception that its leaders are out of touch with the struggles of average people."[16]

Similarly, some businesses are attempting to reduce degree requirements for diversity purposes. Consultancy Bain and Company has urged employers to reduce degree requirements in order to hire more Black applicants. In 2023, Walmart opened some headquarters positions to people without degrees. Some businesses may do this not necessarily for antiracist reasons, but to improve hiring in a tight labor market.[17]

Federal efforts to tear up the paper ceiling also cross the partisan political divide. The Biden administration pushed on this theme in its last year, attempting to encourage hiring practices that downplayed postsecondary certification. For one example: "The Administration launched nine Investing in America Workforce Hubs across the country that are bringing together unions, local governments, employers, training providers, schools, community colleges, and other stakeholders to facilitate partnerships to train and connect workers to jobs in high-demand sectors."[18]

Note that K-12 schools and community colleges play some role in this vision, but not as exclusive guarantors of job credentialing, nor are bachelor's-granting and graduate schools present. The same official statement included this clear assertion: The Biden-Harris Administration is laser-focused on creating training pipelines that ensure all Americans can access the hundreds of thousands of good-paying jobs created by the President's Investing in America agenda—whether they went to college or not.[19]

This effort downplays college for all in favor of a mixed approach. In 2024, then-presidential candidate Harris repeatedly called for reducing college degree requirements for at least some federal jobs: "As president, I will get rid of the unnecessary degree requirements for federal jobs to increase jobs for folks without a four-year degree." Harris's official campaign statement on the economy included this call for a government to "create workforce programs that work for all Americans and strengthen the care economy, opening pathways to the middle class for more Americans that don't require a college degree." Even former president Obama supported the idea, reversing the course he charted as president, praising on social media "a smart policy that gets rid of unnecessary college degree requirements and reduces barriers to good paying jobs," adding, "I hope other states follow suit!"[20]

Meanwhile, Republicans have supported this, as politically attuned readers might expect. A leading conservative periodical, *National Review*, celebrates Virginia's Republican governor's decision to remove degree requirements for state jobs, arguing that "most of what was taught in the classroom has little relevance to job performance anyway." Note their description of anti-paper-ceiling strategies as a kind of disillusionment: "The moment students graduate, we pretend this rigamarole was some tremendous formative experience that has now produced skilled employees. Research shows that students retain little of what they learned, but many employers pretend that having earned a college degree, in and of itself, is a vital qualification for employment. Starting with former governor Larry Hogan in Maryland, state governments are no longer pretending."[21] Rigmarole and pretending: this is the language of an idea deflating, seen as a mistake or illusion.

Donald Trump followed suit on the campaign trail, verbally. As president for a second time, he has not taken action along these specific lines as of this writing, despite his many other moves against higher education. Yet as we noted in the previous chapter, Project 2025, which Trump denounced while campaigning but has apparently embraced while governing, calls for ending the paper ceiling at the federal level: "Minimize bachelor's degree requirements. The President should issue an executive order stating that a college degree shall not be required for any federal job unless the requirements of the job specifically demand it."

All told, we would be wise to anticipate continued calls for ripping up the paper ceiling and thereby further reducing the demand for college.[22]

After decades of building up higher education access to the height of college for everyone, a remarkable movement with major historical impact, America seems to be reversing course. Not only has enrollment dipped, but the cultural consensus around the value of a university degree is breaking up, from cities and companies to state and federal governments. There are political reasons to push against more college, both from the right and left, but also a bipartisan move to tear up "the paper ceiling." There is an economic rationale for improving hiring.

This is both a cause and an effect of peak higher education. When economic and political leaders step back from encouraging more postsecondary enrollment, when they celebrate *not* having degrees, this exerts downward pressure on would-be students applying to colleges and universities. At the same time, the impression that American academia is on a declining trajectory seems likely to reduce popular support for it. The push to reduce degree requirements could echo through the education ecosystem, encouraging K-12 to step back from universal academic preparation. One sign of this comes from one of the leading primary and secondary school leaders:

> Randi Weingarten, president of the American Federation of Teachers, told The Chronicle [of Higher Education] that Democrats "made a mistake" by putting all the emphasis on going to college, because high-school students need more than one pathway to success. More recently, she said, "We've been saying that high school should be a way to prepare you for career and life, not just college prep."
>
> "The fact that 60 percent of students don't go to college right away," she added, "should have been a wake-up call."[23]

We may be seeing a first sign of K-12 stepping back from universal academic preparation in Knowledge Is Power Program (KIPP) schools and the International Baccalaureate Organization. Both, previously known for rigorously preparing students for postsecondary education, have started offering alternatives to college:

> KIPP Massachusetts has tried to adjust to that reality, renaming its "college counseling" team as "match counseling." It also removed the requirement for a college degree from job listings for "persistence advisers," counselors who work with recent graduates to troubleshoot college, career, mental health and financial challenges.
>
> Similarly, the Bronx Early College Academy, which offers International Baccalaureate's diploma program, is also shifting away from pushing all of its students, who are largely from low-income families, into four-year colleges.

Similar changes may be occurring at other K-12 schools. A recent report noted that in one midwestern state, "32,000 high-school students took classes in architecture and construction during the 2022–23 school year, a 10% increase over the prior year, state data show; 36,000 enrolled in manufacturing courses, a 13% increase over the same period."[24]

Unwinding the college for all drive will likely be an uneven and messy process, given the size, complexity, and decentralization of America's education ecosystem and corporate sector. We may well see contradictory movements, with one state trying to expand tuition support while cutting degree requirements for jobs. In a given middle or high school, one guidance counselor might celebrate the skilled trades for their students, while another urges academic careers for the same population. Some individual campuses may enjoy growth while others shrink.

College for all, or college for some, as it seems to be becoming, might take on a political cast if the present partisan attitudinal divide persists. Progressive and Democratic families might maintain that postsecondary educational attainment is an excellent thing and take steps to make sure that remains true for their families, while conservatives and Republicans tend to encourage their family members into the skilled trades. Progressives might celebrate the ability of college and university life to support a wide range of marginalized people and to gradually improve society through teaching and service, while those on the right advocate for would-be students to avoid those dangerous acts of social engineering. We could overgeneralize here, of course, and recall that party affiliation is not the full story for child rearing and education policy, especially when we consider the vast range of human experience and attitudes across hundreds of millions of human beings. But perhaps college-going will not be so much for everyone as for those of a certain politics. It might become even more of a partisan marker than listening to National Public Radio or watching MSNBC.

Public and private funding may step down if the emerging consensus withdraws from college for all. In fact, we may be making a retrograde movement from "college for all" back to the historical precedent of "college for some." That may be the label for a new consensus, or at least a descriptor of increasingly divided public opinion.

At this point in the present volume, we will shift our approach. Having established peak higher education in recent history and explored how it might play out for the next decade through the previous chapters, in the next three chapters, we will open our analytical aperture to see how post-peak academia responds to several of the largest and most unsettling developments confronting America and civilization as a whole. While the following discussions will branch out in new directions, away from the academy at times, possibly making the reader wonder where this book is going, each chapter will always return to postsecondary education. After all, colleges and universities exist within the broader context of a changing world. That world's transformations will impact the academy, and it is our task here to anticipate how those interactions might play out.

We will begin by exploring how the artificial intelligence revolution might reshape the campus.

CHAPTER 4

Automation Comes for the Campus

Palmer Luckey: What will happen in broader academia when clear scientific consensus is that AI-assisted education delivers better outcomes than 3.8M teachers currently do?

Elon Musk: That is already possible.

—X EXCHANGE, FEBRUARY 2025

Artificial intelligence currently inflames higher education. A growing number of academics find AI to be a multileveled threat to colleges and universities. In this view, it may weaken student learning, introduce quality problems to scholarly publication, deskill or replace faculty and staff, accelerate misinformation, and more. Others are inspired by possibilities for individualized learning, AI tutors, enhanced creativity, improved institutional efficiency, lowered costs, and increased access. The subject is quite complex and fast-moving as technological development races along and academia grapples with possibilities.

In this chapter, we will explore those future AI-academic possibilities to see how they might impact our peak higher education scenario. To do so, we will not start with questions of how classrooms engage technology, from blocking AI to changing assessment. Instead, we will begin by situating higher education's AI work within the larger context of AI-driven social transformation. That is where the AI revolution is practically taking shape, and where the technology impacting campuses is formed, before we start adapting or resisting it. Next, we will explore ways AI might play out across colleges and universities.

We will not offer an introduction to AI or generative AI (built upon large language models, or LLMs) in particular here for reasons of space. Happily, there is already a substantial body of explanatory literature available in multiple media.

One further note: for convenience, we will refer to AI as a trend or force. In that sense, we intend to refer to the software itself, as well as the technological infrastructure that supports it, from data centers to broadband networks. "AI" also includes the individuals, social organizations (businesses, think tanks, media outlets), and cultural forces that advance the technology. At this moment, I don't want to go as far as Kevin Kelly and impute agency and life to technology, but I do want the reader to bear in mind that the term "AI" here can describe software applications as well as an emerging industrial ecosystem.[1]

Recent developments in artificial intelligence present multiple potential challenges to the way the world currently works. As of this writing, there is widespread uncertainty about how AI might upend the labor market, either creating widespread unemployment, giving rise to a new swath of jobs, or instead integrating itself into many positions. People are anxious about AI's new abilities to create content and how they can lead to political messaging, abusive pornography, and deskilling or unemployment for creative workers. There are claims for massive social improvement, such as reducing inhumane or boring work, creating enormous wealth and new ideas, giving new access to services, and improving administrative operations. Conversely, we dread economic immiseration, the end of reliable cultural content, people disengaging from other people in preference to AI companions, and the collapse of shared culture and truth itself. In one view, AI will enable us to successfully grapple with global warming by helping us better wrangle enormous amounts of climate data and generating new ideas, while opponents see AI as exacerbating humanity's carbon footprint and environmental devastation.

Some argue we are on the verge of something like utopia, while others warn of disaster or utter human extinction.

Unsurprisingly, AI's potential impacts on higher education have been very much discussed since OpenAI launched its revolutionary ChatGPT 3 chatbot in late 2022. People within and beyond academia have pondered options for tutorbots, easily generated learning materials, personalized curricula, AI literacy, faculty deskilled or augmented, scholarly publishing degraded or more accessible, a boom in student creativity, a loss of real student learning, and a transformation of career preparation. New startups, new and modified services, critiques, guidebooks, policies, and classes have all appeared and continue to flow.

The purpose of this chapter is not to explain new developments in artificial intelligence. Instead, we will explore AI's potential impacts on academia's future seen through the peak higher education lens. We will begin by offering a major caution to the excitement over the technology's rise and potential for civilizational transformation, emphasizing AI's existential fragility and why all planners and observers need to take that into account. Next, we offer four very different futures depicting how AI might impact colleges and universities, based on James Dator's classic generic futures archetypes model. We then apply those mini-scenarios to our broader peak higher education scenario.

One note of level setting before we proceed: This chapter refers to all of current artificial intelligence when using the abbreviation "AI." Generative AI based on large language models (LLMs) receives the lion's share of attention at the moment, which is realistic, given how rapidly and extensively that revolutionary model has developed, grown, and appeared in so many social locations. Yet other forms of AI are still in use and computer scientists continue to develop them, so "AI" here means, well, AI, unless we specify LLMs. We will also, at times, link digital AI to robotics in the physical realm and will name that accordingly.

We will start our discussion at a social level, rather than by focusing on higher education. It is imperative to do so for several reasons. First, social responses to AI form the context for academia's response in direct and indirect or knock-on ways. Second, technology does not reach colleges and universities stripped of all relations and implications. Instead, faculty, students, and staff apprehend digital tools through the mediations of business, culture, and politics. Third, academia has the ability to help shape social discourse around AI through teaching, research, and community engagement.

When people link the idea of existential threat to AI, they tend to speak in terms of AI presenting threats to human survival. The well-worn and apparently beloved cliché is to evoke the lethal robots from the *Terminator* franchise, imagining ways by which nonhuman intelligence and machines would team up to wipe out the human species. Another popular referent is the dark future described by the *Matrix* stories, whereby humanity invents AI, only for the technology to turn on its creators, killing most of the species and turning the rest into enslaved batteries. Less commonly cited but perhaps more interesting is the paperclip maximization problem, which imagines an AI charged with simply creating as many paperclips as possible. Faithful to its mission, the entity makes as many of the little widgets as its supplies allow, then starts grabbing raw materials from elsewhere. Robots seize metals from furniture, appliances, buildings, automobiles, urban infrastructure, and so on, until civilization itself has been consumed to generate a titanic stock of paperclips.[2]

Yet we should reverse the equation, considering the existential threats AI faces to itself, to better prepare for what might be next. While the combination of popular interest, an initial wave of media hype, investors eager to turn a profit on their investments, and some forecasters have all urged us to expect a world saturated with and transformed by generative AI, and this is a possibility, we should also be open to the likelihood that AI could well stumble, shrink, or fail. As we plan as a society, and as academics, for how to respond to this technology, it is important to bear in mind its fragility.

After all, the history of technology is littered with misfires. We can tell the story of progress by noting how many innovations failed to live up to their promise or failed for a range of reasons. The pneumatic tube for carrying messages, the zeppelin, the Second Life virtual world all had bursts of excitement and usage followed by shrinkage into mere niches. Some inventions faded into complete obscurity—older readers might recall eight-track tapes. And some technologies became massively controlled by governments, corralled into narrow, tightly supervised uses, such as nuclear and biological weapons. Artificial intelligence, a technology first developed in the 1950s, has gone through several collapses of investment and interest, often nicknamed "winters." It would be prudent to prepare for another such.

To begin with, the unreliability of generative AI remains a cause for concern. While new iterations, technologies like retrieval-augmented generation (RAG), and new models tend to improve output quality, LLMs continue to emit enough mistakes and unusual responses as to give users pause. For some people and some use cases, this is not a problem. Weird image, audio, or video output might delight the heart of someone who enjoys surrealism. A researcher or creator looking for new ideas may benefit from a variety of materials in brainstorming. But many of us simply require trustworthy returns to our prompts and cannot risk embarrassment or worse from errors. I have previously compared AI to the horror movie cliché of a mad scientist's deranged assistant: eager to help, but not always trustworthy in the end. Not all users are comfortable playing Victor Frankenstein to a hunchbacked Igor. A perception of unreliability can then drive consumer choices, business strategies, and government actions, all of which shape the technologies presented to academics. Faculty, staff, and student attitudes toward AI output quality play a role in how we apprehend the technology in academic contexts.

Meanwhile, beyond questions of technical quality lies a serious economic problem. While investors from around the world have plowed vast sums into AI, no clear business model has yet emerged. This is not from lack of trying, as AI firms energetically attempt multiple paths to revenue, from tiered pricing to freemium models, charging by tokens to the inevitable advertising, yet none have returned a profit. Cloud service giants Microsoft, Alphabet (owner of Google), and Amazon have added

AI to their offerings, but it is not clear that the addition has increased paying business. At some point, external investors, boards, and CEOs may decide that AI is not justified as a cost of doing business and will want restructuring done to either make a profit or cut losses. Such a process has occurred throughout the Industrial Revolution, as Carlotta Perez has demonstrated, from investment in railroads to radios and personal computers. For academia, this means the generative AI companies offer might radically transform, shrink, expand, or disappear.[3]

Another external force challenges the current AI boom. Multiple people, companies, and associations have filed lawsuits against LLM enterprises, alleging copyright infringement. The basis for these suits is that this type of software requires training on enormous datasets (hence the first "L" in the acronym), and some of those datasets included content that had not entered the public domain. LLM creators generally did not ask the owners of such intellectual property for permission, nor licensed the materials, and thereby rests the harm for which plaintiffs seek redress. AI companies can offer a fair use defense, which seems likely to fail, given that each LLM is an attempt to make money. It would be fairly easy for a judge in any one of these cases to order an AI company to pay extensive damages to intellectual property (IP) holders, which would shatter their already weak business model. Alternatively, a judge could order such firms to suspend operations either for the duration of a case or indefinitely, or compel the deletion of some or all of the software in question. Multiple judges could issue different rulings. The result for higher education is, once more, that a given AI product ceases to exist.[4]

On a related point, governments could issue laws that clamp down on the AI boom. Various governments have attempted to do so already. The European Union issued its AI Act in 2024 (although its full implementation may well stretch into 2027) with multiple provisions to regulate, punish, and discourage different types of AI-caused or -enabled harm. The Italian government banned ChatGPT outright for a time, citing privacy concerns, then fined OpenAI over the same. Several American states have considered laws against AI deepfakes. As the technology continues to evolve and as people attempt new uses of it, we should expect additional governmental actions. Further, as different governments use AI in operations, other states may issue policies and laws against them. In short, additional legal measures may constrain generative AI.[5]

Beyond governments, popular attitudes could also alter academic access to AI. For all of the excitement and hype that greeted and empowered generative AI starting in late 2022, the technology has also elicited opposition. Academics and others have issued critiques charging LLMs with a range of problems: deskilling people, producing biased results, producing low-quality output, degrading information search, confusing users into anthropomorphizing software, abusing workers employed in scanning potentially dangerous content, dehumanizing human interactions, crushing creators, committing IP theft, and more. Polls reveal a mix of popular attitudes, including a significant amount of suspicion, anxiety, and dread. An early 2025 Gallup poll found many people anticipating AI would cost jobs and do more harm than good. Media productions evidently using AI elicit criticisms, such as a Christmas 2024 Coca-Cola ad campaign. These attitudes have persisted and may well shape how societies react to AI. We could imagine different populations avoiding the technology or refusing to access goods and services relying on LLMs. Such attitudes could then build into the aforementioned legal or governmental action.[6]

In other words, the triumph of generative AI as a world-shaking revolution is by no means something we should assume. Threats to its thriving or very existence point the way to different future paths the technology might take. It is possible that different threats will impact the AI world at different times and also at different locations. In one year we could see a business fail, followed by a cultural backlash six months later. One nation may pass legislation which imposes strong controls on AI, while another state spends lavishly to attract and support AI businesses and projects. Looking ahead we may anticipate threats to the technology appearing unevenly across various societies and communities. At the highest level we could see AI both advancing and receding throughout the world over time. All of this makes forecasting the next decade quite complex and challenging.

At this point, we can benefit by introducing one established futures method. The University of Hawaii's James Dator developed a four-fold model for categorizing views of the future in 1979 and has, along with other scholars, refined and elaborated upon it since. It has become a staple in the futures field, used and further developed by other foresight practitioners. Dator's model contains a quartet of scenario types, templates, images, archetypes, or generic stories, each describing how big social changes might occur and how we can start to anticipate them. Each is titled by a verb and pointed at the macro level of analysis.

"Grow" describes a future of social growth, which often includes economic expansion, increased energy, more and improved technologies, longer lifespans, and so on. This can also describe related situations where growth is the theme, like a growing nation or enterprise. "Collapse" depicts a society that suffers a reduction along various metrics, even to the point of extinction. Quality of life degrades along that path of decline. "Discipline" refers to a society that (generally) organizes under a (generally) shared ideal. Dator gives the hypothetical example of anti-consumerism, or a shift to a conservation society. I would cite theocracies and authoritarian ideologies, such as postrevolutionary Iran and Stalinism. "Transform" points to a society becoming stranger, with new ideas and practices appearing, new problems resulting, and changes to life continuing.[7]

In my work on higher education's future, I have applied these four to forecasting on multiple levels, from the macro to the meso and micro, due to their accessibility and scaling capabilities. They can apply to a regional higher education sector, a campus, or an academic discipline. The reader at this point may expect us to apply the model to the future of AI, which we can do quickly. Under the Grow template, the AI field continues to expand, spinning off ever larger numbers of applications and businesses, while services improve and use cases proliferate. In a Collapse situation, AI declines from a peak as its economic model frays and businesses exit the field amid a tide of layoffs and closures, pursued by legal cases and punishing regulations. The technology degrades, never solving the quality assurance problem, perhaps falling further when training on flawed, AI-generated datasets. A Discipline AI future suggests new controls, which might appear within the business community as investors demand profitable returns and entities restructure in order to comply. Legal systems shape AI in this future, reducing deepfake and propaganda abuses. Governments and industries take steps to mitigate automation's fallout. Users learn forms of digital literacy to improve their AI usage.

The Transform AI future might break from these in its potential for novelty. We could expect emerging AI models to offer services we do not currently enjoy, such as creating full-scale computer games on demand or providing human-comparable and persistent conversational partnerships. Applying digital outputs to the physical world could lead to literal changes in the landscape as we implement AI-generated and -derived designs for vehicles, clothing, and the built environment. The capacity for AI to work on code could lead to advances in programming. Beyond this looms the specter of artificial general intelligence (AGI), software which can pass for human in serious ways, then advance beyond its creators' abilities. Infusing robots with AI takes us into even wilder realms of possibility, from physically embodied companionbots to security droids and forms we haven't yet anticipated.

Yet we can go further in this application of the four archetypes, especially in our pursuit of higher education's future. We can expand our vision beyond the technology per se and apply the Dator model to the social change driven by AI. More dialectically, we can consider how American society might change as it apprehends AI and as the technology transforms it. To clarify the results of the exercise, we can take the AI industry at its word and assume it has a large, disruptive (in the literal, not Christensen sense) impact; many institutions and groups struggle to turn the technology to defend their position and social order. I would also like to offer two competing Collapse scenarios, since that framing can generate opposing outcomes.

Grow. AI helps drive social expansion. The economy improves as productivity rises with the help of AI efficiencies, and new, AI-backed businesses expand and become richer. Health care, transportation, governmental administration, and other fields become more productive and effective. More people have more access to more services, from education to law, health care to professional development. Gross domestic product (GDP) rises. This is net growth. Similar to the industrial revolutions, every AI advance caused some businesses to shrink or fail, yielding substantial unemployment. Yet the growth in jobs was greater, with new professions emerging to help make the AI revolution work, leading to an overall improvement in the Schumpeterian "creative destruction" pattern. Culture experiences something of a renaissance as AI enables more production and new forms. Gaming, video, audio, and images are Grow, especially as new talent (who could only do this work with AI help) floods in. AI's impact on the climate crisis has become a net positive. While training LLMs requires a great deal of energy, it's less than it once was, thanks to efficiency improvements. Meanwhile, climate scientists, government officials, corporations, and others use AI to improve climate mitigation and adaptation strategies and operations.

Collapse 1. Generative AI collapses like the Metaverse/Web 3.0 or Second Life did, toppling from a peak of investment and excitement down to occupying just a small niche in the world. A combination of forces could make this happen. Judges in copyright cases rule against one LLM provider, then another. Investment starts to drop. Public attitudes become more skeptical, and active resistance grows. Businesses reduce their AI offerings. OpenAI goes broke. Generative AI still exists, but only for specialists on the margins.

The AI catastrophe's social impacts spread. The loss of billions of dollars in investment ruins some careers, but also causes problems for other investments, leading to more projects beyond AI falling apart. AI professionals suffer widespread unemployment. De-AI-ing government and business becomes a painful chore, which some AI gurus grimly work at to pay their bills. Popular attitudes against Silicon Valley sour, with users dropping away and some major firms losing value. The Chinese government punishes AI leaders in various ways, mostly through career endings. The downfall of AI further injures that nation's troubled economy, which might tip things toward social unrest. Activists who saw generative AI as a climate threat, flush with success, turn their attention to other enterprises they see as worsening global warming: airlines and fossil fuel companies. Educators generally stop teaching with or about AI, outside of computer science classes.

Collapse 2. The implementation of AI at scale causes many social problems, beginning with the degradation of the labor market. Some current workers find their hours reduced to part-time and/or their work deskilled as AI takes up more functions. Others are laid off as AI largely replaces them, albeit with some humans to wrangle and check for quality. Management and owners of AI firms see their value soar as their companies do, while actual AI hiring is paltry, further exacerbating income and wealth inequality. Outside of AI companies, many businesses struggle with losses as they fall behind in an automation arms race or shut down when AI-enhanced firms outcompete them. GDP fluctuates, not yielding an overall growth curve.

Governments struggle with the crisis, trying to maintain social services increasingly in demand while tax revenues run low. Politicians are split, with some opposing AI, urging higher taxes on AI companies and the rich, while others seek the support of those same actors. Political campaigns and government communication regularly use AI-generated content. Cultural production suffers as studios lay off talent and replace them with AI teams. Audiences split on the results, leading to a decrease in purchases and audience share. It becomes a popular diversion to spot content flaws in games, movies, podcasts, and books.

Overall energy demands for AI functions grow, even as new configurations reduce their electricity and water demands, because the requirements for quality output demand more and more computational runs, and AI usage keeps rising. Popular antipathy toward greenhouse gas emitters settles on AI firms, leading to attacks on data centers. Researchers make the case that AI is worsening the climate emergency, and this claim gets increasing public traction.

Discipline. Society splits in two, based on attitudes toward AI. Generative AI users and supporters gradually build out services and implementations throughout the world, evolving protocols and practices, with use. AI opponents carefully carve out "no parrot" and "Clippy free" zones and lifestyles. These attitudes become ideologies that spread throughout society, from politics and economics to culture and relationships. Large administrative systems are reconfigured to adhere to one side or the other. For years, this ideological divide plays out to various degrees of visibility. Government and business services might proudly proclaim their use of AI as an aid to user experience, while creatives boldly offer 100% no-parrot certificates on their wares. Youth subcultures rise, fall, and change based on performative and practice AI attitudes. The rise of AI-enabled robots makes one's position on the divide even clearer. In the climate change world, the divide is stark. Pro-AI researchers and officials rely on AI to analyze sensor data, generate models, and create new forms for climate mitigation and adaptation. Anti-AI people cite climate impact as a major reason for their position and actions.

Transform. The rollout of generative AI and its knock-on effects increasingly make society stranger as institutions and practices destabilize. An AI-assisted robot renaissance sends bots all over the lifeworld. New forms of government operations appear, such as digital twins of politicians, artificial characters of officials. AI-generated content increasingly appears through state publications, not without incidents. The business world is more chaotic as new customer service and workplace practices appear, mutate, or disappear. New businesses and types of companies appear as AI services proliferate. Productivity climbs upward, yet a big churn exists with business startups and closures. Personal relationships with AI, then with AI-enhanced robotics, proliferate while remaining controversial. Lonely people, from children to retirees, spend more time with automation and less with other humans, especially in person; cohabitation occurs, and the humans demand privacy ("It's nobody's business what my bot and I get up to!"). Complaints about humans "logging out of society" rise, leading to bot-shaming. Less intensively, people use AI characters as avatars or fronts for digital situations, then for offline ones, with avatars answering doors and telepresence robots rolling into offices. Various bots serve religious needs, from advice to spiritual leadership. AI-generated cultural works proliferate and become stranger, a new wave of surrealism. New kinds of art appear in movies, body modifications, architecture, and comics. AI-assisted neural translation of human dreams, the thoughts of locked-in people, and of animals begin to change our conception of ourselves. AI-generated climate action is occurring. New designs for wind turbines, solar panel sites, buildings, and geoengineering appear.

Now that we have a broader understanding of AI's social possibilities, we can directly extend them to higher education. Within the Grow scenario, we might expect that colleges and universities successfully grapple with AI as they did with earlier technologies, such as calculators and the World Wide Web. AI becomes one tool of many in classes and other campus operations. Similarly, it is a subject of research in many disciplines, starting with computer science, of course, but also throughout the social sciences and the humanities. We teach, use, and research AI critically and also for its role as an economic and cultural accelerant.

Things are quite different in the two Collapse models. In the first one, postsecondary education generally steps away from the declining AI enterprise, although fields led by computer science continue to study and teach it within their part of the overall intellectual framework. After all, computer science continued to work on AI during a series of AI winters. Campus IT departments no doubt sigh in relief at one less massive technology to support at scale. Faculty, staff, and students opposed to AI are pleased by the outcome, while academics who envisioned a positive transformation for postsecondary institutions are disappointed.

In contrast, under the Collapse 2 scenario, colleges and universities research and teach AI extensively, but largely as a way to give students a better chance in a worsening career market. Political science, business, economics, government, media studies, information studies, environmental studies, Earth science, and other disciplines teach and research AI's chaotic effects on their fields of study, especially as they prepare students for careers in those troubled areas. Some academics protest the impact of AI on worsening climate change, while nonacademics might criticize campuses for working on that (perceived to be) destructive technology.

The Discipline scenario describes a strong divide in higher education, as academics (again: faculty, staff, and students) take up opposing views on AI. Academic units and entire institutions may diverge on this score as positions stabilize and practices become routine. Curricula separate over AI, with some courses of study emphasizing learning without AI as a form of humanism or classical study, while others integrate AI as a way of preparing students well for an AI-shaped world, where a significant number of careers seem likely to use the technology. Pedagogy splits similarly, with those following an anti-AI practice blocking the technology at the network level, in classrooms, in syllabi, and in assignments. Those adhering to a pro-AI discipline integrate AI across all of those levels. The world of research experiences a schism to some extent, with publishers, editors, laboratories, archives, libraries, and more issuing policies for or against AI use. Some individuals make their stance visible through content declarations, social media commentary, and arguments against their opponents.

We should be clear that such an AI divide would not be an entirely new development. Historically, academics have taken up divergent positions over new technologies, starting perhaps with Socrates's opposition to writing in the *Phaedrus*. More recently, we have seen divides on how best to use—or avoid—the World Wide Web, mobile devices, social media, computer gaming, and more. It is therefore unsurprising that we have already experienced academic controversies over the best use (or avoidance) of AI. Emily Bender and colleagues warned us of anthropomorphization in their famous 2021 "stochastic parrot" paper. Academics such as Maha Bali and Siva Vaidhyanathan have taught and published critiques, warning us of the technology's dangers. Jennifer Sano-Franchini, Megan McIntyre, and Maggie Fernandes organized a movement to resist AI among writing instructors. In contrast, we find Ethan Mollick, José Bowen, Eddie Watson, Brent Anders, and others urging higher education to embrace AI for many benefits.[8]

It is possible that what results from this Discipline divide is the emergence of AI as an information technology stratum within the academy. It does not become widespread or global in use throughout academia, like web pages, learning management systems, or smartphones have become. Instead, AI becomes something akin to e-books: enjoyed by some, shunned by others. It is available as an option in certain circumstances and not in others. Campus infrastructure supports AI, but usage is optional, much as with the combination of e-books and print books maintained by IT and libraries. The analogy breaks down, of course, when we consider the far greater scope of AI as compared to e-books, its vastly larger potential for social disruption, but we might nonetheless experience a parallel, should the Discipline scenario offer an accurate forecast.

Alternatively, the two-tiered Discipline model might eventually come to some kind of integration. One thinks of the popular distillation of Hegel's philosophy of history, with a thesis (generative AI, in this case) eliciting an antithesis (anti-AI discipline) and ultimately yielding some kind of synthesis. Perhaps all users, including those opposed to AI, will become accustomed to some instances of the technology in various parts of life: voicemail decision trees, web search results, recommendation systems, and automated agents. AI-generated art could gradually cease to be remarkable or even noticed and become part of the visual culture universe, as we have already seen with computer-generated graphics, CGI in films, digitally edited photographs, as well as digital filters for images. Critique might have a significant influence as working conditions improve for those people laboring on AI guardrails, deepfake laws reduce offenses, users stop anthropomorphizing the technology, and software trains on datasets more representative of the full range of human identity and experience. The two tiers of Discipline gradually coalesce into one, both in society and among academics.

To return to our final Dator scenario, our Transform model opens up a wide range of possibilities for higher education. As the world becomes stranger under AI's impact, academics might emerge as more trusted and stable guides to a transforming society. Academic research can play a role in the outside world, producing new ideas and instances of software and hardware, sometimes leading to business spinoffs. Within campuses, the emerging human–bot relationship becomes the subject of concern, with faculty and staff anxious about bot-connected students (and faculty as well as staff) becoming too dependent on software. At the same time, we seek to turn such relationships to good ends, with improved mentor-bots and research assistants or colleagues. Institutional leaders increasingly fear external competition in the form of commercial bots offering education with more convenience and at lower prices.

At this point, we can at last turn our attention to AI and the overarching theme of this book, the peak higher education scenario. Our discussion so far gives some options for the next decade against which we can examine interactions with an academic sector moving on the wrong side of peak.

The AI and society Grow scenario may offer certain advantages for colleges and universities. A growing economy can be good news for campuses receiving state and federal funds, as well as all seeking philanthropic support. AI-derived efficiencies could enable institutions to reduce costs. On the enrollment side, if a given school supports students in AI study through pedagogy (using AI in teaching) and curriculum (teaching about AI), and if the nation perceives that to be both true and significant, then we could see student applications rise. On the reputational side, AI research and public scholarship might give an institution some attention in the public mind, which might be good for enrollment, public funds, and donations. In other words, Grow could push a campus back toward peak.

However, Grow could also weaken academia. An AI industry that improves its output quality and its external reputation may well offer educational bots that prove appealing enough to compete with colleges and universities. They might begin with a focus on a particular topic, such as physics or music theory, then gradually expand into others, much as the language-learning app Duolingo has moved into mathematics. Such a bot would be available at all hours and, if AI development progresses, become quite personable. Students could become personally attached to a tutorbot as a friend. K-12 schools might license them to supplement in-class learning. For higher education, a convivial, always-available tutor might prove a serious competitor if the price point is low enough. That might prove a Christensen-level disruption.[9]

Collapse 1 might not have much impact on higher education, as it is largely an external phenomenon, although the extent to which a campus relies on external AI (commercial, not locally run open source) for operations will expose it to some friction and loss. In contrast, Collapse 2 could push colleges and universities further downslope or back toward peak, depending on circumstances and strategies. A chaotic economy not enjoying net growth would likely depress public and private funding. The traditional wisdom that enrollment rises with unemployment numbers might not occur, as it did not occur during the 2020 recession. A lack of clarity about the college-to-career pathway, given AI-driven economic uncertainty, may depress academia's perceived value. On the other hand, an AI recession might comport with pre-2020 tradition and see a flood of applicants, especially if college looks like a safe haven in comparison to the AI-racked workplace. Institutions could build on that last point, providing the certainty of professionally vetted knowledge.

A Discipline world might see individual colleges and universities mapping onto different student populations at the institutional level. A pro-AI campus that embeds the technology throughout its operations, from teaching to back-end administration, would appall would-be students who practice the other discipline; the reverse would also likely bear out. A campus divided by AI ideologies, with schools, divisions, and departments taking up different positions, might approach students in a more complex or nuanced way, offering a richer set of AI experiences. That would entail its own challenges, of course, starting with computing infrastructure management.

Transform offers some more possibilities we now recognize. An increasingly chaotic world might decide to benefit from an academia it perceives as relatively durable and wise. The humanities might resurge as chroniclers and analysts of emerging cultural forms, attracting more students. Academics contributing to the AI revolution through open-source work and other forms of research and development might improve the sector's reputation. Conversely, the world of Transform also holds the possibility of the tutorbots we've discussed above, perhaps in new forms we do not currently recognize. The popularity of companion AIs like Character.ai suggests we might see software representing personalities with which some engage.

Overall, the impact of AI on American higher education may well depend on a campus's strategic orientation to the technology, from official direction at the presidential and provost level to classroom teaching and student support. We now see several possibilities where AI could depress colleges and universities further, eroding enrollment and popular opinion. Conversely, we might climb back up toward peak by engaging with AI in certain ways within certain social responses to the artificial intelligence revolution.

We can conclude on two points. First, it should be clear now that AI represents a powerful force capable of significantly, if not massively, reshaping the academy as well as other structures within the rest of civilization. AI might not be as salient as the invention of steam power or the taming of fire, as some have excitedly observed, but it remains a major force applied to colleges and universities. In this chapter, I have used the language of revolution to describe the technology's impact, and I chose the term carefully. AI can represent an overturning of hierarchies and operations within the postsecondary ecosystem. It is, as we have seen, capable of destruction as well as innovation. It is a revolution that threatens established ways of thinking and doing while making possible new forms of praxis. In terms of the peak higher education scenario, AI can give campuses a push as they slide down slope, accelerating their decline. The technology might instead offer ways for academic institutions to change that negative trajectory.

Second, in this chapter, we have touched on a major problem that AI is starting to either address or exacerbate. Climate change may, as we have seen, give academics a powerful reason to critique or oppose the technology as its demands for electricity and water soar. Members of a campus community may also determine that AI is a useful force for understanding or mitigating global warming, from its large-scale effects within the earth's system to how we renovate campus buildings and what curriculum we teach. The climate crisis on its own terms is a vast challenge, larger and more impactful than AI, and higher education is just starting to engage it. How might the academy respond through our teaching, research, outreach, and campus operations? Will global warming hasten peak higher education's institutional decline or offer ways to rethink the postsecondary ecosystem? That rising engagement is the subject of the next chapter.

CHAPTER 5

The Anthropocene Is Here, Ready or Not

Professor Bernard Quatermass: The will to survive is an odd phenomenon. Roney, if we found out our own world was doomed, say by climatic changes, what would we do about it?

Dr. Mathew Roney: Nothing, just go on squabbling like usual.

—*QUATERMASS AND THE PIT*, RELEASED 1967

In the previous chapter, we explored the potential impacts of one major trend on society and higher education. We saw how artificial intelligence portends possible changes at a grand scale with powerful implications for peak higher education. In this chapter, we'll examine another trend, a different source of transformation that takes place at an even greater level: what climate change could mean for the peak higher education scenario.

As a problem, climate change possesses a daunting scale and enormous complexity. That scale, its difficulty, and the manifold ways it intersects with civilization combine to potentially justify a new category of thought, not merely an object but a *hyperobject*, in Timothy Morton's formulation. We therefore do not have space to explicate the extensive scientific literature by which we understand global warming, nor to address its deniers and would-be debunkers, nor to survey in detail the growing scholarship from the social sciences and humanities exploring impacts on politics, society, culture, and psychology. Instead, we will proceed here by accepting the international scholarly consensus on human-caused global warming and refer readers to its large and growing explanatory literature in multiple media. My own contribution to that corpus, *Universities on Fire*, offers an introduction to the topic and pointers to resources. More to the point, that book provides the background for this chapter, but is not required to make sense of what follows.[1]

It may be useful to set the stage by noting exemplary developments in climate change. The melting of Greenland's glaciers is accelerating. One recent paper "estimate[d] that children born in 2020 will experience a two- to sevenfold increase in extreme events, particularly heat waves, compared with people born in 1960, under current climate policy pledges." Those pledges assume a 1.5-degree centigrade temperature rise over pre-industrial levels will be achieved, yet major financial institutions have stated that they expect twice as much heating—3 degrees. The year 2024 saw temperatures at a modern peak—1.55 degrees.[2]

In what follows, we will sketch out a model for the many points of interaction between academic institutions and climate change. Next, we will outline several ways by which global warming can contribute to our peak higher education scenario. To the extent that popular attitudes become more committed to climate action, colleges and universities that refuse to visibly demonstrate such a commitment may see student interest decline. Conversely, institutions that draw on communities opposing climate research and action may lose students if the latter perceive the former to be too engaged in the topic. At a different level, climatological impacts on civilizational infrastructure in the many forms of natural disasters, economic damage, political instability, and so on, could drive academia further down the post-peak slope as well. The well-established uneven impact of climate change on marginalized populations may reduce their representation in academia, leading to fewer students, staff, and faculty from underrepresented groups, exacerbating inequities. Such climate harm can strike campus populations and infrastructure, of course, causing human suffering as well as exerting pressures on an institution's physical and economic sustainability. Further, as global warming exacts tolls on society's abilities to provide well-being and safety, perhaps leading to crises and emergency situations, society might reduce its support for some aspects of higher education, or for the academic enterprise as a whole.

It is important to bear in mind that global warming does not intersect with academia in a simple, singular, or straightforward way. Instead, impacts and responses will take place, and are already taking place, on multiple levels. Moreover, a given institution's situation (geographical, cultural, political, financial) and identity give each one distinct forms. In this chapter, we will discuss the topic primarily from a macro perspective, breaking out cases when possible.

We can start by analyzing climate change's impact on higher education into three levels. To begin with, perhaps the most obvious such dimension is the direct effect on an institution's physical plant, grounds, and community. Much depends on circumstances, of course, as some campuses are exposed to saltwater flooding while others exist in arid areas, for example, but there are general effects to consider, such as the overall rise in temperature. Scientists forecast rising numbers of and higher temperatures in heat waves. This is especially problematic when accompanied by humidity, as that yields high "wet bulb" temperatures, which are dangerous to humans due to the difficulty the body has in shedding excessive heat. Certain areas of the United States are more prone to wet bulb dangers, notably the southeast. Conversely, aridity increases the chance of fires, as it dries out combustible material, such as underbrush. Such fires have become disturbingly familiar, like the Los Angeles ones in January 2025. Arid areas are likely to expand around the world, including much of the United States west of the Mississippi River. In both wet and dry heat, rising temperatures can worsen air quality in general. Additionally, excessive heat can impact travel by increasing air turbulence for aircraft and by overheating train rails. Storms of all kinds, from hurricanes to tornadoes, are likely to become more dangerous and frequent, as we saw with several campuses racked by unusually strong hurricanes in the Southeast during 2024. On campus, we must consider buildings overheating, members of the community having health issues due to air quality and heat, rising costs of air conditioning, fire damage, and more.[3]

Meanwhile, sea level rise presents further challenges to the physical aspect of colleges and universities, and will likely accelerate as major parts of the cryosphere (think Greenland and Antarctic glaciers) weaken and melt. Sea level rise immediately threatens coastal properties and populations, where people have historically tended to cluster. Dangers include bigger and more frequent floods, subsiding land, and saltwater infiltrating into fresh groundwater. Early signs of this are already apparent, as we have already seen Louisiana's coastline reduced and insurance companies reduce coverage of properties elsewhere along the Gulf of Mexico and the West Coast. Indeed, the attention insurance companies pay to climate change and their energetic remaking of policies in response should convince everyone of the problem's urgency: "Nearly half of all homes in the U.S., 44.8%, are at risk of severe or extreme damage from environmental threats, according to a new report from the Realtor.com® economics team. Almost $22 trillion in residential real estate is in danger of flooding, wind damage, wildfires, heat, or hazardous air quality." All of these present stresses and threats to campus grounds, from lawns to buildings, sports fields to infrastructure, and drinking water. They threaten human safety and wellness in numerous ways.[4]

A second level of climate threat involves the campus in its immediate biological setting. Global warming will adjust—is already adjusting—biomes around the world, as the aforementioned temperatures rise, water changes, and natural disasters occur. This entails some animal populations on land, in water, and in the air migrating to new areas. Certain plants will die off in some areas that can no longer support them, and others will appear for the first time in different locations. In short, a given region's mix of flora and fauna will increasingly change. This yields new patterns for diseases, depending on their position within an ecosystem, possibly giving rise to epidemics and pandemics. To pick one example, the chikungunya virus has already started spreading, with cases appearing in the United States, causing the U.S. Food and

Drug Administration to approve a vaccine for it. Ticks migrate to different areas, bringing with them infections such as *Rickettsia parkeri* rickettsiosis. The academic population, as well as its local community, faces disease risk. Beyond diseases, the plant and animal ecosystem that a given academic institution supports and lives with may alter, such as with certain plants and trees weakening while new species appear or are better suited to the area, literally changing the look and feel of a college or university. This can impact institutions as well as neighbors who rely directly on their biome, such as farmers and agricultural programs, as well as tourist sites.[5]

Beyond the environmental and physical impacts lies a third level in the form of the effects of human decisions and actions: our politics, social responses, and mental reactions to the crisis as it ratchets up. We can anticipate a wide range of these, from government policies, business strategies, consumer shopping, religious practices and beliefs, mental illnesses and attitudes, new content and forms for storytelling, and more. Such responses can exert themselves on academic institutions, starting with various forms of climate policy and direction: requirements to use certain types of energy, incentives to implement some technologies, and prohibitions against climate-related actions. Local, state, and federal governments can issue policies and laws that might support or oppose climate actions, and thus impinge on a college or university. Community actions independent of governments can also impact a campus, such as protests and boycotts. Businesses that colleges and universities work with, either locally or nonlocally, can change their offerings in response to consumer choices and political pressures. Of course, any one of these actions or attitudes can change over time or be contradicted by others.

Each of these three levels can influence the others. Increasing fires may elicit local government actions, for example, and a transformed environment has psychological impacts. The pressures we described in the first two levels can lead to still another human action: immigration at increasing scale, as people flee dangerous areas, notably those especially punished by high wet bulb temperatures, climate-accelerated disasters, or both. A campus inhabiting such a zone might experience its local community starting to dwindle, or it could have a harder time attracting students, faculty, and staff who feel less than enthusiastic about moving to a climate danger zone. A campus in a safer area may consider supporting climate immigrants, either by in-person hosting or online teaching. Governments from the local to federal level might require or incentivize schools to undertake such humanitarian actions, perhaps with the assistance of nonprofits. Of course, they could also do the opposite, prohibiting or sanctioning academics for doing climate migration relief work.

Faced with such a triple threat, academia can anticipate its challenges and respond strategically. Such institutional responses occur in several domains. I have previously identified them as actions in the physical campus, its infrastructure and population; the academic research enterprise; our teaching mission; and work with communities, both local (town-gown relations) and national or global. We can break these down now in some detail.

We have already outlined global warming's challenge to our built environment, and we can see that in our grounds: damage to buildings and grounds, injuries to people. Yet we can also identify ways by which colleges and universities can adapt to these threats, and also try in some way to mitigate the crisis. We can re-source our electrical power supply away from fossil fuels to renewables, either by building projects on campuses (solar, wind, geothermal, hydro) or outsourcing to nearby providers. We can modify current buildings and rethink new construction to reduce the carbon footprint according to established standards such as Leadership in Energy and Environmental Design (LEED) and Passive House. Depending on the location, a campus might seek to protect or harden itself, such as by building floodwalls, clear-cutting acres of flammable foliage, or elevating structures on pylons. More drastically, an institution's leaders may decide to move their operations to another, safer location.

There are many more options available for the physical campus in the global warming context. A given college may decide to expand its information technology services in order to give academics alternatives to carbon-spewing in-person travel. Digital tools can also analyze campus data and create strategies in response: temperature and humidity sensors, electricity usage, times of power draw, and so on. Alternatively, another college might reduce its information technology (IT) use to reduce its part of the digital world's large carbon footprint. Institutions can change food service to provide more plant-based options, which reduce the methane and CO_2 emissions caused by America's meat- and animal product-centric diet. A school can replace vehicles (cars, shuttle buses, carts) that burn fossil fuels with hybrids, then electric vehicles (EVs). A similar policy encourages visitors to use EVs when traveling to and parking on campus through fees or tactically located parking spaces. A campus might expand its trees in order to sequester carbon. More ambitiously, a school could site a direct air capture installation in order to draw CO_2 down from the local atmosphere. The options in this domain are extensive.

Academia has already had a major climate change impact in another domain, research. The Intergovernmental Panel on Climate Change (IPCC) document shows just how much university research contributes to humanity's apprehension of the global warming hyperobject. Institutions can build on that historic and current research mission, expanding the amount and quality of scholarship we produce. (Recall that while the usual understanding of "we" in such discourse is professors, the reality is that staff and students also conduct research.) Universities and colleges can support more of this work across the disciplines, which sometimes requires some structural support and political cover. As we have touched on, all branches of the academic world can produce new understandings of the crisis. The sciences clearly play a leading role in grasping climate change, from environmental science to chemistry, hydrology to physics. Engineering already plays its role in creating new structures to cope with new stresses. The social sciences help us see human responses, from politics to sociology, economics, and psychology. Then the humanities contribute still more investigative capacity, exploring climate change in religious and historical contexts, while grappling with how we communicate the story through literature and the arts. Any college or university could expand its research accordingly. This means researchers (again, faculty, staff, and students) may need support in terms of professional development, library collections, situating climate research in terms of professional recognition, potential political cover, and more.

In a material sense, colleges and universities may contribute to protecting or duplicating research objects and sites, endangered by global warming: archives or archaeological materials threatened by excessive water or heat, and natural sites mutating due to temperature or migration. Some of those objects might not survive, and so institutions face supporting researchers through those problems. Does the academy invest in ways of preserving the focus of research, such as funding improved storage for rare archives or building protective barriers around archaeological sites? Do we turn to the digital world, meticulously cataloging and duplicating digital twins of these objects? As with our own campuses, do we consider moving research materials to safer locations? Other research challenges are political, as politicians and activists critique or threaten academic researchers; institutions should defend the latter from the former.

Beyond research, teaching is core to academia's purpose and constitutes another domain for climate engagement. Similarly, it's one that's already active to a degree. Some college faculty teach global warming in various fields across the curriculum, from the natural sciences through the humanities. I have elsewhere referred to climate change teaching and learning as the new liberal arts because of this interdisciplinary dimension. We should anticipate more of this teaching to occur as more instructors seek to engage climate, and especially as students demand it. We can go further than classes, developing minors, majors, and graduate programs in multiple aspects of the subject: climate mitigation, decarbonization management, climate storytelling, global warming policy, and so forth. At a small level, climate micro-credentials could suit some learners, depending on their situations. Overall, as with research, professional development is in order for some instructors who want to do more. That entails institutional support: departmental or program funding, assessment in terms of professional standing, and, as before, potentially political backing.

There are other serious questions inherent in how we do climate teaching. Older methods of lecture and drill-and-kill practice have limited utility. Instead, we can turn to more active and creative pedagogies to teach these very complex topics, such as problem- or inquiry-based learning. These methods can carry a student across disciplines and other intellectual boundaries as they explore, letting them produce learning through their own arcs of progress. Elsewhere, simulations and games are established ways of engaging students while teaching complex systems; we already have a growing body of such materials, from tabletop games like Daybreak and Climate Fresk to the En-ROADS simulation website. At the same time, instructors and support staff will face the challenge of how to teach and support students who suffer from various forms of climate anxiety and trauma. This may result from direct experience of damage and disasters as well as from awareness of the vast problem. The number of these students will generally increase over time as the crisis develops. How we support these students—how we honor their mental states without retraumatizing them—is a matter for very careful pedagogical research and development.

Beyond the classroom extends another domain for academic climate change engagement, that of community and public climate work. Local collaborations offer many possibilities, such as sharing cooling shelters, jointly constructing solar arrays, and building (and maintaining) seawalls benefiting both town and gown. Academics can conduct research in local communities, such as sociologists examining how a city responds to increasing wet bulb temperatures or economists tracking how businesses conduct decarbonization. Collaboratively navigating the crisis can be very fruitful. At the same time, of course, town-gown friction can occur. A climate activist academic unit might irk an opposed local enterprise, or the reverse, with community climate activists criticizing their neighboring campus for perceived inaction. Cross-cultural misunderstandings and basic human friction have long been the bane of campus-community relations, and we should not expect them to be absent from this work.

Furthermore, beyond doing research in communities, scholars can share their work with the world. This can take the form of public education, teaching people apart from enrolled students via public presentations and events. It can also occur with academics performing the role of public intellectuals, sharing their research to influence policy and behavior nationally or globally. Media, old and new, can play roles here, with members of the academic community taking to podcasts or newspapers to share their work. They might lobby various audiences for change. Once more, an institution would need to offer various forms of support to such researchers: technical assistance, media consultations, peer assessment, and so on. This may again include, potentially, political protection.

Beyond individuals performing the role of public intellectuals is an even more ambitious form of outreach: institutions collaborating with each other at a regional, national, or international level. Campuses can connect with each other to exchange information, to share resources, and to pool their climate capacities. There are opportunities for shared curricula and classes. If a given college or university cannot afford to host a climate professional support center, perhaps several can share one, either virtually or in geographic proximity, such as a regional academic climate hub. America's geographic diversity is a strength here, as faculty, staff, and students from an arid region can work with a campus in a very humid zone, as in inland schools learning from coastal ones. Our institutional diversity is also a strength in this regard, as research-intensive universities can connect with community colleges carefully attuned to workforce development, and art schools introduce new storytelling approaches to liberal arts colleges. International possibilities go even further, especially for nations and regions with different approaches to climate change.

In short, academics confronting the climate crisis are exposed to threats in multiple ways and have a range of domains within which to respond. The scale of global warming constitutes a huge, historical challenge to colleges and universities. Individual faculty, staff, and students have a world of possible responses. At the same time, institutions face strategic pressure requiring strategic thought and action.

With this sketch of how academia and global warming intersect, we can now return to our focus on peak higher education. Connecting the two involves a great deal of complexity along with huge variations based on individual campuses' distinct characters and capabilities, so the discussion that follows occurs necessarily at a high level. This chapter—indeed, much of this book—invites readers to apply such macro mapping to their circumstances and interests.

We can begin with a level setting in academia today. Based on my research behind *Universities on Fire* and working with thousands of academics since it appeared, climate change is not generally a major concern for American higher ed. There is some action at the early adopter level, as per Everett Rogers's diffusion model (1962): small numbers of faculty doing research and/or teaching, as mentioned above; some presidential commitments to gradual decarbonization, often through carbon credits; food service, anticipating a more plant-based diet; and campus planners and architects, looking ahead decades to make campus buildings and operations safe and low-carbon. Apart from a few leading campuses, such as Dickinson College and Duke University, climate is largely not a strategic commitment for colleges and universities. The subject rarely appears in professional discourse, given its huge importance. This was true before Donald Trump's return to office. After his campaigning against climate action and taking steps against federal global warming research and policy, it seems to be even more true. Trump's White House adds more incentives to stay quiet on climate, not to mention on many other issues.[6]

Yet this may change. As climate concerns and activism rise further among the American public, we may see opportunities for colleges and universities. Such a rise seems likely, given the visible and personally experienced ratcheting up of global warming as well as generational differences about the topic, with younger people being much more concerned than their elders. That should drive more climate interest among college students, who may increasingly decide to apply to campuses with clear reputations for climate action. Colleges and universities with opportunities for students to take climate action—to study, to research, to prepare for climate jobs, and so on—may enjoy rising demand. On the other hand, students may choose not to apply to, or not to persist in studying at, colleges and universities that do not offer convincing signs that they take climate action seriously. This may be especially true of traditional-age students, given the age differences for climate attitudes. A visible lack of climate-themed curricula and programs, combined with few climate actions on the campus physical layer, could yield a public profile that increasingly becomes an application and enrollment liability. We noted earlier how central enrollment is to the overwhelming majority of institutions' financial viability. This should be a problem to anticipate.

Further, colleges and universities presenting reputations as disengaged with global warming may suffer additional challenges along these lines. They may experience a difficult time hiring faculty and staff, especially as the younger generation ages into such positions. This could also yield challenges in retaining climate-committed faculty and staff as the planetary crisis worsens. Some might leave an institution for more climate-engaged ones, or exit the academy to try making an impact through some other pathway.

Returning to the multiple domains model sketched above, we might also anticipate difficult town-gown relations when campuses appear in such a light. Obviously, that relationship difficulty depends on the local politics of a given community, with conservative areas being less disappointed in their scholastic neighbors than progressive ones. Yet right-left framing might not hold in all cases, especially as the climate crisis intensifies and people who might be otherwise anti-progressive find themselves adapting to hard reality. We can easily consider hypotheticals. Imagine county members furious at a college that doesn't allow them into cooling shelters. Think of a school with a large commuter population, such as a community college, and how local climate activists might criticize campus reliance on gas guzzlers, or not doing enough to facilitate mass transit for students. Consider a campus that builds very visible, physical protections against disasters, such as constructing a prominent flood barrier or setting up a helipad for emergency fire support. How might its neighbors respond when they suffer from water or fire, in the face of a protected academic institution? In other words, worsening community relations and hiring caused by changing climate attitudes present challenges to colleges and universities.

Such a cultural shift might worsen the reputation of higher education as a whole. Let us posit the possibility that over the next decade, American society changes in a way whereby climate denial retreats and climate engagement grows, especially as the crisis advances. If the nation's colleges and universities appear to be sitting out the fight, will public opinion about the sector sour further than we have seen in chapters one through three? This might occur if a substantial number of postsecondary schools appear not to be committed to climate action, or if an elite institution wins negative media attention for a climate story: elaborately refusing to decarbonize campus travel, for example, or cruelly punishing climate activists. Some might see academia as retrograde, a negative form of our conserving mission. Or we might appear to be in denial of a crisis too much of a hyperobject for us to grapple with.

Yet the situation is not so clear-cut as "jump on the electric climate change now, or else your institution may suffer." A second climate-peak higher ed scenario rests on the possibility that climate denial may persist for years and also have significant political, cultural, and economic power. We do not have time to dive deeply into such thinking here, but can note some of its established drivers and subthemes: anti-intellectualism; opposition to experts, often along class and education lines; opposition to science itself, at times based on strong religious faith; a belief that climate action is bad for the economy; a perception that climate action is anti-progress (see chapter six); and a conviction that climate stress and damage are overblown or will arrive too far off in the future for us to engage fruitfully with it in the present. Some of those have deep roots in American culture. They have been evident, even at times decisive, in recent American elections. It is possible, and perhaps likely, that such attitudes will decline in the next decade, as noted earlier, but they might take a long time to dwindle, especially if they receive significant political and financial support. We can imagine a nation largely committed to burning fossil fuels and resisting any climate mitigation or adaptation. Leading climate journalist and activist Bill McKibben described this:

> You can imagine a world where the U.S. builds tariff walls around its borders, prevents the easy development and spread of technology like EVs and heat pumps, and manages to become an island of internal combustion on an increasingly electrified world.[7]

Or, as climate scientist Michael Mann put it:

> With the reelection of Donald Trump, a candidate who has flaunted his desire for autocracy—aided and abetted by a Republican-controlled Congress that will not constrain him with guardrails—the United States is now poised to become an authoritarian state ruled by plutocrats and fossil fuel interests. It is now, in short, a petrostate.[8]

It seems unlikely that the United States would become such a total regime, with all decarbonization efforts erased in favor of a retrograde fossil fuel dystopia, but we can see powerful forces striving to make it true. It could happen in enough structural and geographic locations and over enough years to impact academia. This pro-carbon world would make college and university climate action more difficult, of course. We can project it through our domains model, starting with it becoming harder to take climate actions on campus. Funding for renovations and EV charging stations would become scarce, for example, and permitting renewable energy sources on or near campus would become more challenging. Climate research may elicit hostile reactions from public officials or activists; protecting research sites may be daunting. Teaching climate could backfire if a student body is disinterested or opposed to the subject. Negative community reactions are easy to imagine: carbon boosters blocking a new wind turbine or denouncing the school for not purchasing CO_2-burning cars from local dealers. So much depends on awareness of the local environment and the student recruitment market. Academics who advance climate work in the teeth of McKibben's world could push their institution farther down the slope.

The escalating damages of the climate crisis over the next two decades may yield additional effects on American higher education through what disasters do to our civilization and its infrastructure. It is well established that climate damage falls unevenly across populations. Broadly speaking, the wealthy are far better protected from fire, flooding, and so on than the poor. In the United States, the top 10% and especially the 1% have far more access to shelter, effective property insurance, transportation, medical care, and political sway than do the remainder. Black, Hispanic, and Native Americans generally tend to lack the resources enjoyed by whites and Asians. Girls and women are more likely to suffer from climate damage. In short, the climate crisis reproduces social inequities. To the extent that academia wants to address them through student recruitment, along with faculty and staff representation, the effects of global warming may make this more difficult. Individuals and families who can ride out storms are in a better position to attend college than those whose lives are shattered. The financial damage wrought by climate change will fall harder on the poor and those lacking inherited wealth. Absent strategic interventions by colleges and universities, representation of the marginalized and minorities could well drop as a result of the climate crisis. A more inequitable campus then reproduces those injustices.[9]

Additionally, to the extent that climate change physically impacts campuses, human suffering results. To repeat: We should envision students, faculty, and staff potentially being injured or killed by worsened storms, fires, floods, poor air quality, and other dangers. The physical plant also may take damage from those causes, from buildings to vehicles, electrical infrastructure to grounds. Academic operations may slow down. The financial costs of such harm may press on the budgets of institutions already operating on thin margins or at a deficit. Preventive measures are wise, but can also be costly: additional insurance policies, improvements to buildings, alterations to landscapes. Paying climate costs may drain funds from elsewhere, especially if nonprofit or public support is unattainable. These physical threats may push institutions further downslope.

At a broader level, we should anticipate how American society may respond to climate stresses. Much depends on how destructive the next decades will be. There are many physical factors involved in making such an estimate, such as the degree to which major glaciers melt, notably in

Greenland and Antarctica; the deployment of geoengineering efforts; the potential for Arctic clathrates to loft methane into the atmosphere; how much carbon and methane humanity emits; and the potential for volcanic cooling. There are social and political factors as well, notably how seriously we treat the crisis. IPCC reports offer several pathways of varying degrees of catastrophe. It is reasonable to forecast that natural damage may cause social and political changes, such as governments organizing defense and relief programs, consumers altering purchasing and savings habits, and emergent attitude shifts toward climate change and everything it touches. We have already noted the chances of states of emergency and mass climate migration. In such a chaotic situation, we may ponder how nations will view higher education, and how that could shape the peak scenario.

Perhaps Americans and the rest of the world will turn to colleges and universities for support in the crisis. After all, many people have for generations seen academia as a trusted source of knowledge. Our teaching, research, community, and public work can contribute to how humanity navigates the Anthropocene. Yet postsecondary education might not fare so well overall. A nation focused on emergencies might view some of higher education as of secondary importance. Perhaps there will be pressure for research and courses of study deemed practical and germane to the struggle. Civil engineering, agriculture, electrical engineering, and meteorology might come to the fore, for example, while other fields drop back in terms of enrollment and investment. Public institutions might lose state and federal funding when those governments decide that direct climate action is more urgent: building pipelines to bring fresh water to arid areas or those whose water tables are in crisis, repairing roads and dams, expanding first response capacity. Academic dissent from government actions could reduce public support for institutions. Would-be students might vote with their feet to work directly on climate emergencies, rather than studying about them in classes.

Things could become more chaotic still. Consider the possibility of more natural disasters: increased and stronger storms and heat waves killing hundreds of thousands or more, the collapse of food systems, coastal regions flooding, and a growing area of the earth's surface too dangerous for human habitation. People might lash out at those they view as responsible for the crisis or benefiting from it. Protests against and attacks on fossil fuel companies, their bankers, and their political agents could drive a crackdown on climate activity or dissent in general. Popular support for, or acquiescence in, the current political economy could fracture, with new or resurgent ideologies taking hold of the body politic.

All these forces could impact higher education. To what extent will outraged populations hold academia responsible for the crisis? After all, we graduated students in fields like petroleum engineering, finance, political science, philosophy, government, computer science, and economics, which might appear to have helped make the crisis occur. In this view, our teaching and research contributed to making greenhouse gas emissions happen, to formulating neoliberalism or extractive capitalism, to seeing the earth as a supine subject for human desires, and to colonialism. We could face a reckoning on those accounts. Alternatively, academia might appear to have come too late to climate awareness and action, and will seem worthy of being set aside or sanctioned as a result. Will students reject our curricula for being outdated and irrelevant to the current crisis? Put another way, if society cracks at the seams under Anthropocenic pressure, colleges and universities might face a chaotic struggle for survival.[10]

Confronting these climate change possibilities can be daunting and even terrifying. It requires interdisciplinary and transdisciplinary thought and the building of cross-silo relationships. It should be evident at this point that the climate crisis can exacerbate the institutional decline our peak higher education scenario has outlined. At the same time, strategies of positive engagement with global warming may give new life to our campuses, from how we design and operate physical plants to our teaching, research, and outreach. This is a very difficult project to undertake in many ways, but it is not one we can choose; humanity and the earth have already chosen for us, and so it is upon us to rethink, reinvent, and act.

The past two chapters have broadened our discussion of peak higher education, and the next will expand the picture even further. That is because the AI revolution and the climate crisis encourage us to reflect deeply on our human project. In addition to working out the details of how a given college or university responds to those two forces, the combined challenge encourages us to ask what ideas, politics, cultural tendencies, and social mechanisms brought us to this dangerous, even catastrophic moment. One such school of reflection takes us backward in time, examining the generations of industrial revolutions that built our civilization and produced both artificial intelligence and anthropogenic climate change. That reflection then looks ahead, anticipating where we might take things over the next century based on how we got to this point. Our sense of human identity, our notion of growth, and our faith in progress are at stake, and two divergent schools of thought about them are emerging. What those two ideologies are, and the roles of our schools in both developing and implementing them in the daily life of a college or university, is the subject of the next chapter.

CHAPTER 6

Academia and the Struggle for Humanity's Future

Technology is the glory of human ambition and achievement, the spearhead of progress, and the realization of our potential.
For hundreds of years, we properly glorified this—until recently.
I am here to bring the good news.
We can advance to a far superior way of living, and of being.
We have the tools, the systems, the ideas.
We have the will.
It is time, once again, to raise the technology flag.

—MARC ANDREESSEN

Growth for the sake of growth is the ideology of the cancer cell.

—EDWARD ABBEY

After exploring how artificial intelligence and the climate crisis might impact American higher education in its post-peak moment, we will now widen our analytical lens even further. Here we consider not only what might occur in the future, but also emerging ways of thinking about what comes next. It is the argument of this chapter that two such opposing ideologies are starting to grow and will likely inform the collective imagination and decision-making for many of us. Those competing ways of understanding and acting in the world involve and impact academia's future in important ways. In fact, our ways of thinking about peak higher education are already starting to show signs of this developing future-ideological conflict.

These emerging schools of thought are only partly futuristic. They stem from divergent views of two centuries of industrial revolutions and the resulting sense of progress. One school holds that the best way forward is for humanity to double down on progress, advancing forward with even more energy. Its opponent urges a halt, arguing that progress has come with terrible costs, and that leaning into progress would repeat and worsen grave problems. In the following pages, we will outline each ideology in some detail, then see what they might mean to colleges and universities. A reader who has been with us as we explored developments in higher education's institutional structures may be surprised by what follows—a brief move to the history of ideas and popular culture—but we will shortly return to practical academic applications.

One should note that these are *emerging* ways of thinking about the future. Neither has an accepted name as yet, although we will suggest provisional ones. Neither school of thought has attained the hegemonic scope of, say, Maoism in postwar China or various forms of Western Christianity in Reformation Europe. Both ideologies are also developing at the moment, sprouting offshoots, internal divides, and new ideas. Each intersects with other ideas, cross-pollinating and mutating. This chapter attempts to identify them in the present moment, then to forecast how they might change and have real-world impacts.

We begin with a very ambitious, macro-scale assertion. For the past roughly two centuries, humanity has experienced a literally extraordinary transformation. Circa 1800–70, civilization broke away from the lives and conditions we had known for millennia, based on many material metrics. What we now think of as modernity took off, gradually then steeply, albeit unevenly, around the world and across societies. We can describe this change as the outcome of one or several major movements: one or several industrial revolutions based on a series of technological innovations and their promulgation through nations, the onset of modernity, the emergence and popularity of the idea of progress, the eventual results of the Enlightenment, breakthroughs in medicine and public health, the extension of the scientific revolution, the appearance of new forms of capitalism, and European colonialism's global rise and peak. There is some argument over when the divergence occurred. At the earliest, some date it to the late eighteenth century and Britain's first steps with steam power. Others push the takeoff into the later nineteenth century with the rise of the Second Industrial Revolution and its combination of mass production, standardization, and a torrent of technological and economic inventions. For our purposes here, we can bracket out the precise dating in order to emphasize the main idea of an unprecedented break in human development compared to previous millennia.

To support this assertion, we can cite many metrics. Total gross domestic product (GDP) rose dramatically, starting with the leading industrial nations of Britain, France, Germany, and the United States, followed by Japan. GDP per capita similarly grew. This stands in contrast to how historical GDP was generally flat for previous centuries, as far as the available evidence shows. For another measurement, we can look at the number of people throughout history. The total human population stood at circa 300 million by the year 1 CE and gradually rose over centuries to 1 billion by around the year 1800. Growth then rocketed up after that, reaching two billion in the 1920s, three in the 1960s, four in the 1970s, then up to eight billion in 2022. We can add other metrics, quantified to various degrees of detail, depending on evidence availability and inference, such as human life expectancy, poverty rates, energy produced, governmental power projection, calories in diet, and democracy. Again, the pattern repeats: a long sweep of history being largely flat or at best incrementally rising for millennia, only to be succeeded by a sudden growth spike beginning around the year 1800.[1]

Readers might advance three objections at this point. First, that the sudden takeoff involved a great deal of inhumanity and suffering, from poor industrial working conditions to colonialism's dispossession of many people, the imposition of European religions over other beliefs, multiple wars of conquest, the height of slavery in the Americas, and more, or worse. These are quite legitimate criticisms, and we will return to them shortly, as one of the two ideologies we're exploring is predicated on addressing them. They do not undo the fact of massive civilizational takeoff, but complement that account by showing its horrible costs and effects. Second, readers might contest the choice of these particular metrics. For example, GDP is only a rough measure and does not do a good job of capturing quality of life or economic nuances. The projection of state power can be celebrated, but also understood as a cause of suffering. These are important points and have been made throughout the period under discussion. As with the preceding objection, they play a major role in one of our ideologies, and we will return to them shortly. Third, we can contest many points about the grand historical timeline just offered, which can appear too simplistic. Different nations and populations experienced this rise in separate arcs, for example. A focus on post-1800 innovation downplays centuries of preceding development. We can grant these and point to a burgeoning historical literature on this point, but for our purposes here, we would like to retain the big picture idea: that human civilization experienced an unprecedented transformation over roughly the past two centuries, in just seven or eight generations. Even if it's flawed historiographically, that immense change has shaped (among other things!) attitudes, which we are now in the midst of receiving and transmuting into new ways of looking at human development.

To that end, we can now turn the historical gaze around and point the idea of progress forward. Where might that striking upward growth curve take us in the future? Using a simple extrapolation, the trajectory suggests that we should expect continued growth across multiple metrics, from lifespan to wealth and accumulated knowledge, but this is by no means certain. That extraordinary growth has recently slowed or stalled at several points, notably the demographic transition we discussed in chapter two. Medical care and public health efforts continue to extend our lifespans and quality of life, but we also see the spread of new and resurgent diseases, which cut that back. Transportation reached heights with bullet trains and the Apollo missions, yet supersonic civilian air travel failed, and human spaceflight remains bound to lower Earth orbit. Increased availability of food has reduced starvation and helped grow billions of people, yet also led to multiple negative side effects, not to mention a massive diet industry. We have access to the greatest amount of knowledge in history but remain afflicted by magical thinking, pseudoscience, misinformation, industrial-scale rumors, and multiple forms of scams.[2]

So, what now? A growing discussion over the continuation of that growth curve is emerging around the world. In response to the extraordinary progress of the past two centuries, we now see diverging attitudes developing into complex and diverse models of the two hundred years to come. In other words, given 1800–2000, what should we do with 2000–2200? Out of this vast ferment, we can identify a pair of broad systems of thought, opposed to each other very strongly, and taking shape swiftly. One of these complexes of ideas is committed to continuing and escalating the progress wave, to expanding humanity's footprint even further, and improving the quality of life to new heights. The other system calls for a halt to that takeoff, for shifting human energies away from growth and instead toward civilizational repair and redesign, either because it is the ethical way forward or because we will have no choice in the matter due to emerging circumstances. Each of these ideologies is grounded in previous discussions taking place across multiple domains, from economics to literature and power politics, dating back to the eighteenth century. Both are starting to surface in political arguments, popular culture, and scholarship.

The first ideology views those two centuries of rapid growth as not only historically extraordinary but also a boon to humanity and worth doubling down upon. That industrial revolutionary era of continuous innovation and increasing development is one to celebrate, refine, and extend. In this view, the construction and extension of modernity is an epochal triumph and one to build upon. It sees the four industrial revolutions as a civilizational launch pad from which humanity can rocket away to even greater heights. In terms of future studies, we can view this as an optimistic and deliberate instance of James Dator's Grow model, as described in chapter four. For the sake of convenience, I have provisionally labeled this ideology *hypermodernism*, adding the Greek for "over" or "beyond" to one word for the past two centuries of growth.

We can think of this hypermodern future model in terms of the metrics we cited above to describe the modernity boom. From the launch point of circa 1800 to the present day, the human lifespan has extended, doubling from roughly 30 to 40 to the late 70s. If we continue that pattern into the future, lives lasting longer than a century become normal, and two-century lifespans become, eventually, unsurprising. The past boom saw massive improvements in medicine and public health, so if we continue to run those arcs upward, we should expect more diseases to be controlled or eradicated, and injuries better controlled. We could imagine cancer cured at last, and people bouncing back from wounds in short times. Human knowledge expanded immensely during the industrial and postindustrial eras, as did educational attainment, so the next two centuries should see us learning ever more. The sciences, social sciences, humanities, and arts should progress by leaps and bounds, and people study for more years, perhaps truly to the extent of lifelong learning. We go much further with multiple forms of human flourishing, coming up with new cultures and ways of living. Put another way, the Cold War divided humanity into first, second, and third worlds in order of political alignment as well as descending civilizational development. We can imagine a *zeroth* world ahead of the first, even more advanced than the greatest achievements of the first.[3]

Science and technologies clearly developed rapidly in the past two centuries, from steam to atomic power, railroads to human spaceflight, Newtonian physics to quantum theory and dark matter, printed books to virtual reality, cures by bleeding to computational biology. The pro-growth futures school anticipates more such advances, including new scientific and technical revolutions and their embodiment in the physical and human worlds. For example, hypermodernists expect public and private space exploration to continue energetically as machines and humans spread through the solar system, then reach out to nearby stars. Our industrial base might move from Earth's surface and crust and instead function in orbit, benefiting from unfiltered solar power and a lack of gravity, allowing us back on Earth to re-green the world. Present reality affords grounds for this as a second space race proceeds, led by China, NASA, and SpaceX, with many other nations and companies joining in. For hypermodernity, automation should progress much further, with AI reaching the point of sentience, superintelligence, or even the fabled Singularity, creating alien intelligences in silicon that complement, and then surpass our own. Meanwhile, robotics increasingly becoming capable of many human and nonhuman tasks, present so widely in the world as to become commonplace, like animals or other people, taking all kinds of forms.

In the life sciences, hypermodern humans not only live longer and more safely, but with a higher quality of life. We might modify our bodies to this goal, from adding more artificial components to improve or extend functions to genetic engineering. The old term "cyborg" simply describes ordinary humans in this emerging world, given the prevalence of artificial items in our bodies and the redesign of the human form. We develop new plant and animal species, as well as resurrect some extinct ones. The biosphere expands by adding more animals and people in total, including more "animals" and "people" in newly engineered, cyborg, or otherwise novel forms. Humanity's footprint is far larger than it was in the relatively benighted 2020s. Taken together, our whole human enterprise controls and generates more energy. In the twentieth century, the Soviet astrophysicist Nikolai Kardashev published a typology of future civilizations by how they created and used energy, a framework which astronomer and public science communicator Carl Sagan then developed further. In this system, a Type I society accesses the energies of an entire planet, while a Type II controls the energies of a star, and a Type III, the output of a galaxy. Humanity at present stands around a Type 0.7, depending on measurements and assumptions. Hypermodernists would see us reach Type I and work energetically toward Type II over the next two centuries. Along the way, perhaps we will surround our sun with vast fleets of solar collectors or crack the secret of safe fusion power.[4]

Popular culture offers many imaginative examples of such futures. Science fiction (which is also a creation of the past two centuries, with

Mary Shelley's *Frankenstein* appearing in 1818) describes a rich array of possibilities, while also giving us insights into relevant challenges. For example, *The Expanse* novels and television series (2011–21, 2015–22 respectively) outline a solar system explored and settled by humanity, where large-scale engineering projects are underway. We might see the television series *Star Trek* (first broadcast 1967) as offering a positive vision as key to hypermodernism, with its portrayal of an advanced human race spread among the stars, enjoying accelerated science, and, at times, a very progressive social order without money or physical want. Beyond *Star Trek* is Iain Banks's series of *Culture* novels and shorter stories (1987–2012), which describes a galaxy of worlds, natural and artificial, where grand and humane technology maintains humanity in what is at its core something like an interstellar utopia. People travel easily through space, enjoying immense lifespans and leisure. There is, in short, a utopian flavor to hypermodern thinking along with a sense of epic grandeur. The Chinese writer Liu Cixin gives us a sense of this in his *Death's End* (死神永生), the conclusion to his popular *Remembrance of Earth's Past* series (2006–10): "And now we know that this is the journey that must be made by every civilization: awakening inside a cramped cradle, toddling out of it, taking flight, flying faster and farther, and, finally, merging with the fate of the universe as one."[5]

Nonfiction futures work has also anticipated such an epoch. For example, Alvin and Heidi Toffler envisioned orbiting factories above a greener Earth, all driven by an accelerated capitalism. In contrast, Aaron Bastani imagined what he called *Fully Automated Luxury Communism*, where automation yields a much more egalitarian and excellent life for all. The Tofflers perhaps find an echo in *The Expanse* series, while Bastani resonates with the *Culture* sequence. The transhumanist idea, developed in articles, books, speeches, startups, and numerous projects, plays a part in this vision of the future, with its emphasis not just on modifying the human frame but improving it and creating new forms for people. Uploading consciousness into computational substrates constitutes one strand of such an evolving, technologically advancing civilization. Journalist Kevin Kelly asks us to think of an "extropian" worldview, one always pushing for improving the human condition, especially through science and technology, as a kind of vast struggle against entropy.[6]

Going even further along this line, the longtermist movement offers another example of nonfiction hypermodernist thinking, but one based on a much longer timeframe. This theory looks ahead not just a mere pair of centuries but across millennia and more (hence the name), to a time when humanity sprawls across the galaxy in a megacivilization in a nearly godlike state. We can think of that view as calling for humanity to reach not just Kardashev's Type II, but to aim for Type III. Longtermists see this potential future as the acme of human history, a glorious and unparalleled achievement. It is therefore our duty in the present day to devote our energies to best realizing that goal, akin to medieval workers contributing their efforts toward building a cathedral, the completion of which they might not live to see. Attaining that vision should animate our lives and collective work.[7]

At this point, the reader may react with skepticism to one or several of these points as seeming unlikely or impossible. Longtermism has received criticism for being so focused on its distant goal as to dismiss present-day problems, such as social justice or climate change. In its model, we can do more good now by helping make that very long-term future happen, compared to aiding people in the present. That is where we see longtermism's intellectual roots in the effective altruism movement, a philanthropic project for the very wealthy and often technologically immersed set, encouraging them to plow their gains into present projects most likely to yield that eventual cosmic goal. Effective altruism received a major hit with the conviction and imprisonment of one of its stars, Sam Bankman-Fried, for very present-oriented bitcoin fraud. Beyond that individual, might such futures thinking represent indifference, cruelty, and even disaster to our time?[8]

Other wealthy figures have espoused hypermodernist ideas. Leading investor Marc Andreessen published a "Techno-Optimist Manifesto" in 2023, calling for a rededication to technological advancement backed by capital, with ambitious aims. It offers many hypermodernist-friendly points. For example, there is this call for expanding the human population:

> We believe our planet is dramatically underpopulated, compared to the population we could have with abundant intelligence, energy, and material goods.
>
> We believe the global population can quite easily expand to 50 billion people or more, and then far beyond that as we ultimately settle other planets.
>
> We believe that out of all of these people will come scientists, technologists, artists, and visionaries beyond our wildest dreams.
>
> We believe the ultimate mission of technology is to advance life both on Earth and in the stars.

Similarly, Andreessen calls for more and more energy production:

> We believe energy *should be* in an upward spiral. Energy is the foundational engine of our civilization. The more energy we have, the more people we can have, and the better everyone's lives can be. We should raise everyone to the energy consumption level we have, then increase our energy 1,000x, then raise everyone else's energy 1,000x as well.

While the manifesto received a great deal of mockery, it remains the expression of a very influential person, an investor with a broad reach. We might consider it a key document for the history of emerging hypermodernism.[9]

Taken together, hypermodern ideas might appear unsettling to some of us, such as modifying the human body at scale, using computers to house some form of consciousness, or devoting our era toward an incredibly far-off and possibly implausible goal. Readers may also note that there are contradictions and tensions under the hypermodernist tent, such as between communism and capitalism. Others could argue that the preceding framework is painfully simplistic as a way of understanding two (or more) centuries of human history to come. Other critiques may appear, such as: How does such an aggressively ambitious project resist reproducing present and past injustices and inequities—for example, by settling other worlds and echoing the history of European colonization? Would a posthumanist effort to redefine humanity backfire in horrible ways, or cost us some crucial essence of what it means to be *homo sapiens*?

All of these points have some validity. As with any ideology, what I've been calling hypermodernism elicits criticism and opposition. An especially ambitious way of thinking about the future requires more space and consideration than we can fully provide in the present book. Yet some of those critiques appear in the form of an opposed and emerging ideology, one which we will now outline. This school of thought poses a question that exactly reverses hypermodernism's fundamental idea: What do the next two centuries look like if we reverse civilization's course, and instead of growing, we plateau, then *contract*?

Asking that question might seem perverse or outright offensive, given the immense boons the past two centuries have yielded, as described above. Which advances might we shudder to give up: antibiotics, GPS, jet travel, longer lifespans, the birth control pill? Why on Earth would we want to cut GDP or reduce literacy? The school of thought I'm provisionally referring to as *demodernism* argues that we need to rethink these questions and more, because it's the right thing for humanity and the planet. Moreover, we might not have a choice in the matter.

Demodernism is a combination of two James Dator futures archetypes, as described in chapter four. It contains elements of both Discipline and Collapse. Demodern thinking requires a new organization of society, hence the discipline model, in this case, a massive turn away from the progress narrative. It also describes a collapse in various ways, from a voluntary reduction in civilizational operations to an involuntary decline or crash.[10]

To explain: we can find elements of demodernist thinking across the nonfiction world, from journalism to climate action to technology writing. Leading climate journalist and activist Bill McKibben offers one argument in his 2019 book *Falter*. There, McKibben agrees that the past 200 years have yielded progress, but they also kicked off catastrophic global warming, which is becoming an existential threat to humanity. Therefore, the only ethical or even practical response we have is to address that crisis, which means drastically and immediately reducing greenhouse gas emissions, notably CO_2 and methane. This entails a massive restructuring of society's energy infrastructure through a shift to renewables, including energy production, storage, transmission, and use. Such a process may see total energy and, as a result, economic output fluctuate or pause for the transition.

McKibben goes further. Considering the two centuries of industrial progress, he finds that they were also marked by a legion of crimes against humanity. European colonialism seized much of the globe in that period. Repeated genocides scarred the species. Hideous inequities by gender, race, religion, and more occurred. Yes, we have since made progress on many social fronts, but so much remains to be done. Repairs and redress have begun to various degrees, such as the process expressed by South Africa's Truth and Reconciliation Commission, yet the vast problems require much more work. McKibben invites us to recognize our progressive achievements and then to divert the terrific energies which made them possible to repairing the world. We should pause that trajectory of epic growth, in other words, in order to ethically pay its true costs. Given how far civilization has come, we can choose to do this now, deliberately and wisely.[11]

Also from the climate change world, in *This Changes Everything* (2014), Naomi Klein asks us to commit to truly revolutionary transformations of our society. Climate justice becomes central in her account, with an emphasis on Indigenous people as victims of fossil fuels, protectors of the environment, and guides to a better world. Klein takes a more Marxist view than McKibben, calling for overturning capitalism as she sees that system as primarily responsible for making the climate crisis happen. To do so, to create new ways of living after both capital and global warming, we should consider how to support human flourishing in a precarbon way, which implicitly downgrades our economy. Klein is skeptical of technology as a tool for her cause, criticizing, for example, geoengineering to reduce global warming as a wasteful distraction.

In one significant passage, she overturns a nearly mythic symbol for space exploration. The famous Earthrise photograph of the entire world seen from the moon (taken by astronaut William Anders in 1968) has become an invitation to rethink the earth beyond political boundaries. When pilots and astronauts have seen the earth in that perspective, they have sometimes reported a nearly mystical sense of the precious nature of the world and the importance of continued space exploration. Frank White coined the term "overview effect" to describe this vision as a positive source for perspective and inspiration. In contrast, Klein views that symbol as a crude misunderstanding of the real earth, one which leads us away from on-the-ground realities.

> When environmentalism went into outer space, adopting the perspective of the omniscient outsider, things did start getting . . . awfully blurry. Because if you are perpetually looking down at the earth from above, rather than up from its roots and soil, it begins to make a certain kind of sense to shuffle around pollution sources and pollution sinks as if they were pieces on a planet-sized chessboard. . . . And . . . any acknowledgement of the people way down below the wispy clouds disappears—people with attachments to particular pieces of land with very different ideas about what constitutes a "solution."[12]

That supremely technology-enabled vista removes from view the practical details of watersheds, biomes, and local environments. Instead, it is far better for us to set aside that artificial overview and to return to the planet's surface and get to the business of repair and restoration. Similarly, in a contemporary article, Jordan Bimm called out the overview effect as both a result of and a call for militarization and colonization.[13]

From a different yet related angle, Donna Haraway has written and imagined a future where people reduce our total population by focusing on making kin, not babies. Those kin may be human or nonhuman; the point is to lower reproduction, re-engage with already living humans, and to become closer to the natural world. Haraway's future includes people repairing industrial-era damage to the earth through science, careful construction, and rewilding nature. Humanity's footprint gradually shrinks, and our pressure on the world becomes gentler. We cease to be conquerors and evolve into fellow members of a complex ecosystem.[14]

We can find demodern thinking in economics as well, starting from the assertion that our current economic system has produced and exacerbated the climate crisis and other problems. As a result, we are seeing more efforts to rethink the current economic order. Kate Raworth's "donut economics" model calls for a kind of political economy that allows for growth, but only under a series of constraints and limitations. We would throttle back from excessive production, which drives the earth over a series of planetary boundaries, then construct a political economy that guarantees a quality-of-life baseline for all. The "donut" is the literal sweet spot we can occupy by avoiding exceeding those boundaries and by failing many people. Others call for clearly stopping economic growth, sometimes called a steady state economy. Here, the pressure to keep expanding GDP stops in favor of a more thoughtful, more just organization of economic life. Related to these ideas is the circular economy plan, one which emphasizes the reuse and recycling of materials as well as cutting back waste. It keeps items in use and in, well, circulation as long as possible, in opposition to planned obsolescence. These approaches all move the ecosystem to the heart of our political economy, ending the drive for growth at all costs.[15]

In a stronger form of this thinking, we find degrowth economics, which calls for negative GDP, actually shrinking a nation's economic footprint. Degrowth emphasizes noneconomic aspects of life, which people value, from relationships and family to conversation and nonmarketed creativity. Human happiness and well-being become more important than economic measurements. The ecosystem is also at the center of this economic model, as with the preceding ones, but degrowth would end ecologically damaging, yet economically rewarding, practices. Extensive redistribution is a part of this view, moving wealth from the elites to the poorest.[16]

All of these models call for an end to economic expansion, arguing that our wealth has expanded sufficiently to create a good life for all, distributed well. One paper offers this vision of a post-growth world dedicated to planetary restoration: "The restorative pathway would represent a more equitable and resilient world with a focus on nature preservation with vast reserves as a natural climate solution; post-growth economics; societal well-being and quality of life; equality and high levels of education for girls and women resulting in low fertility rates with higher standards of living; more efficient crop fertilizer use; a diet shift with major reductions in meat production; and a rapid transition towards renewable energy."[17]

In this view, there is no need to keep churning out additional stuff if we can guarantee sufficient goods and services for the entire population. Going further, degrowth economics explicitly urge shrinking our production, either directly (by consuming and producing fewer goods and services) or through reducing our total energy consumption. That is one route to reducing the damage humanity's overgrown footprint has wrought.[18]

Alternatively, it is possible that we will not be able to make the degrowth decision on our own because the world is already making it for us. In this branch of demodernist thinking, a massive collapse is already occurring. The human population offers evidence for this. After two centuries of a historically unprecedented boom, we are now seeing a bust, as fertility drops below replacement levels and we draw within sight of peak human population, as we saw in chapter two. Recall that some of that transformation is due to changes in human behavior, but is also otherwise driven by biological changes from endocrine disruptors and declining sperm counts. Global warming offers further proof of how our post-1800 growth spurt is starting to backfire. Further, planetary overshoot models hold that humanity's productivity has pushed key Earth systems into dangerous zones. Increasing ocean acidification would degrade our food systems. The mass extinction of so many species can—among other things—cut into human food systems and health. Running out of needed and nonrenewable industrial and postindustrial supplies (oil, minerals, fresh water, rare earths) can stop growth cold.[19]

In addition, we might get lacerated by disasters that we fail to prevent or cope with, disasters worsened by our civilizational overshoot. Public health experts have confidently expected more pandemics since the late twentieth century, and we have experienced several such, notably SARS, MERS, and, more destructively, COVID-19. In terms of solar weather, a new Carrington event (a massive solar discharge striking the earth) could cripple the digital infrastructure upon which so much of our lives depend. And some humans are quite capable of unleashing new horrors upon the rest of us. I'm a child of the Cold War and am intimately familiar with nuclear and biological threats; these haven't gone away, which should be to our utter shame.[20]

Vanessa Machado de Oliveira argues in a powerful book that these and other crises are, as a whole, inevitable as this elaborate, advanced civilization starts to crumble. *Hospicing Modernity* (2021) argues that the collapse of our achievement of progress is inevitable. We cannot stop it, nor can we see what will succeed it, in her estimation. The costs and wrongs of past centuries, notably colonialism and climate change, are fatal to the whole and cannot be fixed. Instead, the task for the present and near future is to minimize the catastrophe's worst damage, to see modernity off with a minimum of suffering, as the title implies. This will require extensive social transformation, from overturning vast political and cultural systems to doing lots of deep psychological work while rethinking education.[21]

This perhaps fatalist demodern mode is apparent elsewhere. Dark Mountain co-founder Dougald Hine makes a very similar argument in a recent book, *At Work in the Ruins* (2023), urging readers to rethink their lives in this era of descent. He advised our Future Trends Forum community that in many ways, our present task is to live and work so as to leave the best ruins possible for the future. We must be kind to each other as humanity switches off growth and declines into some other situation. Rupert Read, emeritus professor of philosophy at the University of East Anglia, sees the serious decline happening now and that threats are appearing. Sacrifices and losses are forthcoming, and "bullets will have to be bitten." Futurist Ruben Nelson models the decline and fall of what he terms the Modern Techno-Industrial (MTI) form of civilization. Science fiction writer Kim Stanley Robinson, who once wrote solar system-spanning adventures, now wants us to cease space expansion and instead address the earthbound ecological and social crises of our time—exactly the opposite of the longtermist view mentioned above.[22]

Imaginative literature has envisioned various forms of demodernity. Younger readers may have grown up on the recent dystopian boom in young adult fiction, providing many worlds where progress has broken up, reversed, or turned nightmarish. The burgeoning genre of climate fiction often depicts humanity dealing with disasters, shrinking in numbers, or seeing the natural world grow at our expense. More broadly, disaster fiction has been a cultural staple for decades, going back centuries if we consider apocalyptic texts. Science fiction has drawn a bead on the possibility of de-progressing civilization in favor of repair and rebalancing. The "solarpunk" subgenre invites us to imagine a world where climate change spurs us to recreate the world in a better, more humane way. To pick one example, Monica Byrne imagines in *The Actual Star* (2021) a future world where the human population has massively reduced and lives in balance with a much-restored nature. For another, a 1973 Robert Silverberg story imagines a planetary organization landing on Earth in order to undo the damages humanity wrought, whereby team members describe their mission in passages like this:

> "I validate," says Ethel.
> "I unravage," says Oliver.
> "I integrate," says Paul.
> "I devandalize," says Elaine.
> "I unshatter," says Bruce.
> "I unscuttle," says Edward.
> "I discorrode," says Ronald.
> "I undesolate," says Edith.
> "I create," says I.
> We reconstitute. We renew. We repair. We reclaim. We refurbish. We restore. We renovate. We rebuild. We reproduce. We redeem. We reintegrate. We replace. We reconstruct. We retrieve. We revivify. We resurrect. We fix, overhaul, mend, put in repair, retouch, tinker, cobble, patch, darn, staunch, calk, splice.[23]

The demodernist view naturally elicits questions and pushback, and the reader may have already posed some. If civilization downgrades, should we pause science and technological development? What happens to a human culture that has been immersed in dramatic expansion for not just all living memory, but also our formative, recent history? How does such a faltering, to pick McKibben's term, change our senses of identity by self, nation, profession? If we retreat from consumerism, will we be satisfied by noneconomic rewards and pleasures? If we travel less, in order to shrink air travel's significant emissions, than we learned to do in the twentieth century, how might our collective knowledge of people and places decline? How would we transition to a world with fewer services? With what birth pangs would a reparative epoch struggle to be born?

Taken together, hypermodernism and demodernism offer diametrically opposed views of how humanity should proceed. These ideologies are starting to enter into dialogue with each other, although usually to mark out how far apart they are. Hypermodernists charge their opponents with degrading human lives and potential, with unrealistic assumptions about how people value consumer goods and services. Demodernists see their opposite numbers as pursuing ultimately failed expectations of technology, of denying the realities of a finite Earth. These exchanges might seem familiar, as they represent iterations of similar debates. Stanford University's Paul R. and Anne H. Ehrlich elicited controversy with their 1968 forecast of a too-large humanity facing ruin, *The Population Bomb*. The original *Limits to Growth* report concluded on a similarly demodernist note in 1972, using far more primitive models and computation than we now have access to. Earlier in that century, agronomist Norman Borlaug initiated the Green Revolution and expanded the human race, while ecologist William Vogt called for civilizational reduction in the face of overshoot, a point recently put into dialogue by Charles Mann. In the 1980s, economist Julian Simon and biologist Paul Ehrlich held a well-publicized bet over the value of some precious metals, with the former arguing innovation would keep prices low, while the latter believed increasing scarcity would make them more expensive (Simon won). Much further behind all of these debates lies grim Thomas Malthus, writing about nature's ability to control populations in 1798, just before the great industrial takeoff.[24]

There is much more to discover about these competing views of the future. The lineages that we just touched on are both broad and deep, intersecting with other ideas, traditions, and politics. The presence of many ideas within each school of thought deserves more sustained treatment, as they possess depths as well as the possibility for spinning off splinter ideologies in years to come. The sheer amount of imaginative literature underpinning both hypermodernism and demodernism alone is worth several books' worth of analysis. The dialectics of interaction between the two schools, including the possibility of syntheses, are complex and might prove historically decisive. Moreover, looking ahead two centuries offers such a plethora of possibilities for human development that we cannot hope to address in what remains of this chapter. For now, we can pause, having achieved at least an introduction to the dueling ideologies and start thinking through them a bit further.

At this point in our exploration, a reader hoping for more discussion about higher education might be tempted to fling the book aside. Demodernism? Extropians? Interstellar posthumans? What on Earth does this have to do with colleges and universities? Allow us now to connect the dots.

To begin with, signs of this great ideological divide are starting to appear in political and cultural life, which directly impacts higher education. We can see it in opposing ideas about the demographic transition, with a growing natalist movement seeking to encourage more women to give birth. Opponents charge that position with reactionary extremism and invite us to appreciate the benefits of a shrinking human population. The divide appears over space policy, with one side celebrating a new space race to improve humanity, bringing us new knowledge, new material resources, and security against disaster. Against that stand those who view SpaceX as causing environmental damage and the big push beyond Earth orbit as at best a wrong-headed waste of resources better allocated on the planet itself. Science fiction author Kim Stanley Robinson urges us to retreat from space in order to address the earth's problems now:

> Mars is irrelevant to us now. We should of course concentrate on maintaining the habitability of the Earth. . . . If we were to create a sustainable civilisation here on Earth, with all Earth's creatures prospering, then and only then would Mars become even the slightest bit interesting to us. It would be a kind of reward for our success—we could think of it in the way my novel thinks of it, as an interesting place worth exploring more. But until we have solved our problems here, Mars is just a distraction for a few escapists, and so worse than useless.

A similar divide opens up over AI attitudes, as we noted in chapter four. Promoters and enthusiasts see the technology as ultimately empowering humanity, while critics see generative AI as badly biased and exploitative, misusing vast resources and harming lives. The ideological split appears in climate change discussions, with one side urging technological advances as solutions, such as geoengineering and carbon capture, while the other calls for decarbonization, cutting greenhouse gas emissions, and, at times, reducing humanity's footprint.[25]

It is possible that this great debate over humanity's next two hundred years will therefore shape the United States as well as other nations, which is the social, political, economic, and cultural context for higher education's existence and operations. Our governments, businesses, and nonprofits may make decisions stemming from these ideologies, which adjust or transform their offerings. Citizens and consumers may change their behavior in many ways along these lines, which can inflect their attitudes toward higher education, from the decision to apply to a college to funding public universities. A suspension of economic growth in a community, state, region, or nation would hit an institution's endowment. A community college might shape curricula to prepare students to work for local businesses offering advanced amendments to the human body. A resurgent space industry could yield donors who wish to support related campus positions and buildings. All of these choices can impact campuses.

Academics can become involved in the great debate over the future through research and teaching. Leading disciplines already represented in the literature include economics, political science, ecology, history, history of ideas, and Earth science, not to mention literary criticism and media studies. Interdisciplinary research would make sense for the subject, especially as it is already represented in the nature of the debates: an economist arguing with an ecologist, computer scientists working with Earth scientists on simulations. Classes in those departments can teach the subject in undergraduate and graduate courses. As higher education prepares students for the world to come, thinking through this great debate helps frame their understanding of where they will live, think, and work.

Faculty, staff, and students can also play roles in the broader debate. These academics can share their research in a public intellectual mode, entering the public conversation and seeking to influence others. This would represent a continuation of the historical record, as we've noted earlier, where academics contributed to the emerging ideas as writers, public figures, and critics. As the two ideologies evolve, colleges and universities can take part. In fact, the burgeoning debate already addresses higher education, and at least once in an unfriendly way. For example, Andreessen's manifesto provides a list of enemies of progress, which includes academia: "Our enemy is the ivory tower, the know-it-all credentialed expert worldview, indulging in abstract theories, luxury beliefs, social engineering, disconnected from the real world, delusional, unelected, and unaccountable—playing God with everyone else's lives, with total insulation from the consequences."[26]

Perhaps the most powerful impact this argument about the future might have concerns how to configure universities and colleges for the next century. For several generations, American higher education has grown in institutional numbers, enrollment, research output, physical footprint, and wealth, as we noted in earlier chapters. In this context, modern academia has been an expression and advocate of modernity. The academy, in turn, helped make modern society in myriad ways, from the multitudinous impacts of its research to the work of graduates prepared for professions that grow and maintain modern society. For centuries, our intellectual products directly contributed to industrial revolutions, to fossil fuel extraction, to various forms of capitalism, to governments that aided the process of escalating growth. Andreesen is historically wrong, as the ivory tower helped power the technological enterprise he celebrates.

The struggle between hypermodenists and demodernists now asks academics if we would prefer to continue that pattern, or to change it? Will we generate ideas and graduates who accelerate growth or help create the intellectual tools to reverse it? Will the balance of our impact in the world help send humanity into a *Star Trek* future or turn the ship of civilization around in favor of earthly repair and rebalancing? When we look ahead beyond the next academic year, past the four or five years to come in a strategic plan, as we gaze ahead to the next several generations, do we anticipate preparing students and developing knowledge for a world of increasing abundance and advancement, or for a world in decline and collapse?

Our institutions can become functional expressions of those arguments. Our physical campuses are very much subject to this ideological struggle. Some might see growing a college's size, wealth, and impact as part of the hypermodern idea and call for bigger classes, more buildings, and more impressive facilities on the ground. Conversely, others would suspend a campus's growth or start to shrink it, following the demodern theory. The two great ideologies are truly macro positions, but they can play out in meso and micro levels as we make decisions about departments and offices, student athletics and libraries, class sizes and food service, campus vehicles and power supplies. Consider how adding buildings to a physical plant aligns with the growth paradigm. Would a degrowth campus design become desirable, as its community refuses to add to its built environment, resists "edifice complex" gifts, and instead turns spaces over to nature or the local community?

Not all academic institutions face the two ideologies in the same way. Regional and local differences can be powerful, depending on how a given area perceives the divide between progress and repair. A financial hub would have more at stake with the former, while a deindustrialized zone might find itself comfortable with an ethos of no-growth and re-wilding, each forming a social context for a campus. Research universities might find themselves split on the issue, with faculty (as well as some staff and students) producing both demodernist and hypermodernist scholarship. A community college, attuned closely to its immediate labor needs, could find itself shaping its curriculum toward either side, depending on what businesses and government are looking for in their workforce. Institutions that see themselves as closely tied to donors might end up as hypermodernists in order to improve their chances of obtaining philanthropic support. A state university will be tied to its government's approach to the question in deep ways, while a private college might see itself able to pursue shrinkage if its endowment and alumni support it. A religious institution could follow the path its faith marks out in this divide, perhaps choosing some form or analog of the prosperity gospel of growth, or turning to the tradition of simplicity and even poverty.

Returning at last to our main theme, the peak higher education scenario may fit into both sides of the debate. As we said earlier, the long rise of academic institutions up to peak represents the pro-modernity approach of growth across the board. Looking ahead, does the post-peak academy continue to shrink overall, reducing the numbers of faculty, staff, students, programs, and campuses, representing a demodernist view? Such an institution might reduce its standard of care for students, dropping the number of services now offered, or try to improve those efforts to win on qualitative experience when they lose in quantity. Alternatively, or perhaps additionally, do today's colleges and universities commit to repairing the world through decolonizing their curricula, returning lands to Native American nations, researching new ways to ameliorate humanity's impact on the earth, creating new post-growth economic forms, or expanding environment and climate work through teaching, service learning, and career preparation? These are tasks some academics currently pursue, and we might see more of them. A post-peak campus aligning with demodernist thinking might connect with changes to their community, or conversely, disengage from a society still committed to growth and even hypermodernism. Community friction could push an institution further downslope from peak. Perhaps we will come to view our sector's decade of decline as an early expression of the demodernist vision. Perhaps we can reclaim our involuntary shrinkage as a newfound path to managing campus redesign for different demands. Conversely, a reduced academy reflects a society facing its own decline, and we should tailor colleges and universities to best meet that challenging world.[27]

On the opposite side of the debate, academia might throw itself into hypermodernism in an effort to avoid sliding too far below peak. It could seek an alliance with the Andreesens of the world, trying to prove them wrong by demonstrating the sector's enormous intellectual capacity for innovation and development. Such a strategy aims at expanding campus numbers: staff, students, faculty, acres, facilities, publications, patents, documents in the library, and more. It might take a very capitalist form through promoting entrepreneurship, partnerships with growing companies, celebrating wealthy graduates, publishing, and teaching growth-focused ideas. Alternatively, it could aim for the Bastani/*Star Trek* post-capitalist world by generating and teaching new political, economic, social, and cultural ideas for how that might work. We could see campuses applying to become space grant colleges and universities, setting up more business (and even particle!) accelerators on or near their grounds.

If this great debate over humanity's future deepens and if academia engages with it—two big contingencies—then we might see American higher education reflect the divide through its institutions. Campuses might advertise their stance in competition with others: "Join us for the greatest future!" "Study here to prepare for collapse!" At an institution, units, departments, and individuals may contest with each other, much as academics have divided over every era's great concerns. Our question here is how many ways colleges and universities in the peak higher education scenario respond.

Considering the next two hundred years opens the floodgates to other possibilities beyond the large challenges we've discussed so far. For example, in this chapter, we have touched on changes to the human body, which have all kinds of ramifications, from human identity to religious attitudes, new forms of disease, biohacking, and anatomically driven social divides. The COVID-19 pandemic and the resurgence of previously defeated diseases illustrate how public health threats can appear and upend social systems and assumptions. Geopolitics currently presents a wide set of possibilities as the unipolar post-Cold War framework breaks down into multipolarity and the new Cold War between the United States and China develops. Multiple armed conflicts can break out and alter international systems, as the past decade has reminded us. Economic transformation holds other possibilities, including how advanced economies continue to transition away from industry and how we respond to escalating income and wealth inequality. One great question is how globalization proceeds: if it continues, divides into blocs, or retreats. Culture, famously difficult to forecast, offers all kinds of possibilities for art forms and personal connections. There are statistical outlier possibilities, potential black swans, such as the advent of a new religion, damage to the earth from solar weather or asteroids, the appearance of a surprising new technology, or a rogue actor launching a nuclear attack. There are more possibilities still, but they are the province of entire other books. The sheer extent of variables daunts yet inspires the serious futurist.

At this point, we must pause and shift our focus for one more time. In the past three chapters, we have gradually connected the largest ideas in this book with the practical operations of a college or university. In our final transition, the next two chapters will apply our peak higher education scenario to the unfolding operations of colleges and universities. As campuses face the largest forces and questions of our time, from AI to climate change and dueling models of the future, how might academics respond? How should we structure our institutions? In what ways might our core functions—research, teaching, and service—transform?

CHAPTER 7

Managed Descent

Ohio has an overbuilt higher education infrastructure.

—KENT STATE UNIVERSITY PRESIDENT TODD DIACON

How can you tell if your college or university is gearing up for layoffs, and what can you do to safeguard your career? Here are some key indicators and actionable steps to consider.

—RYAN ANDERSON, CRIMINAL JUSTICE PROGRAM AND POLICY SUPERVISOR FOR THE WISCONSIN DEPARTMENT OF JUSTICE; FORMERLY TENURED PROFESSOR OF SOCIOLOGY AND CRIMINAL JUSTICE AT VITERBO UNIVERSITY

At this point, we have carried the peak higher education scenario from its roots in recent history and into the future. We have examined its implications for the "college for all" movement, then explored its intersections with AI, climate change, and emerging ideas about the future of civilization. Now we can shift our focus to how colleges and universities might look if the peak higher education model continues to bear out. What are our options? Which possibilities are available for academics to pursue?

Again, we must remember the contingency of much of this book. What follows here depends on a certain constellation of forces and responses proceeding in ways that carry colleges and universities further downslope from their historical peak. This scenario is not a rock-solid predictor of academia's future, but it may well play out through different strata of American postsecondary education. In this chapter, we advance in the spirit of "as if," if the post-peak condition persists. In that situation, what strategies, redesigns, and initiatives might follow?

I am basing this chapter on several sets of sources, starting with a survey of recent academic responses to stressors. Added to this are many conversations with campus leaders—presidents, deans, provosts, chancellors, along with boards and state legislators—who wrestle with how to preserve their institutions in challenging times. Analogically, I bring in experiences from other sectors grappling with similar or parallel problems, knowing well the limitations of such comparisons. I also add the experience of leading workshops and scenario exercises with a wide range of academics, presenting challenging scenarios to them and working with their responses.

Managed descent is the rubric for this chapter's discussion. We believe in the possibility that colleges and universities may be able to reverse that trajectory, to strive back up toward a historical peak or beyond. Exploring that possibility is the subject of the following chapter. For this one, we are assuming academia continues down the post-peak slope of institutional decline. We expect that colleges and universities will attempt to reorganize and redesign themselves along that path. As we've seen in our previous discussions, the decline is occurring; the question we might ask now is how best to reduce harm and friction along the way.

One relatively painless way an institution can reduce costs is by generating revenue through existing assets. A campus can lease some of its spaces to third parties, such as underused offices or residence halls, when enrollment drops, especially during the summer. These spaces might be for specific events, ranging from scholarly and fan events to weddings. Staff, students, and faculty can share space to free up more. A college or university can also sell some of its physical assets for a monetary infusion. For example, the New School attempted to sell a valuable Manhattan residence. Also, in the Northeast, Drew University has been attempting to make acres of its forest reserve available for development. In the

Midwest, Valparaiso University sold valuable artwork, albeit with opposition. Some campuses can also sell their intellectual property.[1]

At a more programmatically and personally damaging level, program cuts can be a key signal of peak, at least at the level of an institution. These can take the form of ending a degree offering, such as a minor, major, graduate degrees, or certificates and other credentials, if an institution's leadership views them as no longer serving sufficient students to justify them, as well as for other reasons, such as political disputes or interpersonal conflict. Similarly, a campus may combine departments or interdisciplinary programs into fewer units, hoping to save on administrative costs (i.e., to reduce staff time or positions) when perceived demand for their services drops due to redundancy and economies of scale. At a higher level, medium-sized units can combine into larger ones, such as schools or colleges within an institution. Again, an administration may lay off faculty and staff from departments and offices as these measures proceed. As personnel are leading costs for an institution, that is where many administrators will seek savings. There are, sadly, a plethora of examples we can point to. In 2025, Johnson and Wales University announced it would lay off roughly 5% of its staff and faculty. At the same time, Clark University laid off a similar proportion of staff, in addition to 30% of its professoriate. Both leaderships explained their decisions in terms of financial pressure driven by declining enrollment.[2]

Let us look more deeply into such strategies. There are many ways program cuts and mergers can occur. An institution may review programs over time, considering metrics such as the number of majors or minors granted, the number of students enrolled, and the costs of teaching faculty and support staff. A variety of political factors can weigh in, from personality clashes to ideological divides, pressure from a governing body to support from a professional organization. The process can get painful or cruel, with careers blighted. An academic program prioritization method has evolved over the past twenty years, based on the work of Robert Dickeson, whereby an institution compares offerings in order to better allocate resources. At best, this is done with full community participation, a clear process, and with openly available data. It seems likely this methodology and others like it will appear on campuses more often than they currently do if American higher education continues downslope from peak. In a more drastic way, an institution can declare financial exigency, an emergency status indicating existential risk. That declaration allows for radical institutional reorganization. Again, post-peak higher education seems likely to experience more financial exigency cases.[3]

In the range of possible cuts, it is important to recognize the hierarchies within institutions. Tenured faculty are in important ways among the most powerful players on a campus stage, given the protections tenure offers, although they constitute a minority among postsecondary faculty. In contrast, the majority of faculty consists of tenure-track but not yet tenured faculty; full-time instructors working on contracts but without tenure; and adjuncts, hired to teach individual classes on a per-semester basis, known as "sessionals" in Canada. The latter represents the largest proportion of American higher education faculty. Staff also exist on a spectrum of institutional power, depending on their unit and position. Staff usually lack tenure, although some campuses afford librarians that status to different degrees. Some staff, senior administrators, receive relatively high compensation compared to most of the rest of the campus workforce.

Lower-ranked staff and adjunct faculty are the easiest to dismiss; indeed, adjuncts can simply not be hired for another term. As an institution whittles down programs and units, these people are often the first casualties. Cutting tenured professors is a more drastic step, which is why I apply the chess term "queen sacrifice" as an analogy to describe when it occurs. In the game, the queen is the most powerful piece, so a player's decision to give it up is an extremely risky move, only done as a desperate gambit to win the game. By analogy, removing tenured faculty is a sign of serious institutional trouble, a risky gambit aimed at achieving sustainability. As higher ed proceeds downslope from peak, we should expect more queen sacrifices.

None of these strategies would occur without the possibility of community resistance. Some students, faculty, and staff will protest and try to block cuts in the next decades, as they have done historically. Their arguments can take the form of institutional protection, calling for the preservation of programs, departments, curricula, as well as for saving individuals from harm. Preserving campus capacity plays a role here in the form of preserving people for the institutional memory and tacit knowledge they hold. Some cut opponents will also call for maintaining threatened units because their value goes beyond the financial. Instead, they play a key role in an institution's identity or mission. Others will denounce cuts and mergers as an excessive emphasis on financials over the nonprofit nature of most colleges and universities. That view often sees cuts as expressions of a corporate or neoliberal administration.

These arguments can slow, modify, or stop cuts, depending on a given institution's political situation and the resulting process. Their proponents can use them internally to build a community consensus against the administrative plan. Externally, they can stir public opposition and negative media attention, which could embarrass administrators. They can also call for cutting administrative and staff compensation and numbers, charging that remuneration is excessive, following Benjamin Ginsberg's famous "administrative bloat" critique. Alternatively, they can seek new funding sources to protect their programs and people: alumni, philanthropists, and local and state governments. Such resistance could conceivably elicit broader cultural and political debate, raising issues of what society values from higher education. Recent history offers plentiful examples of such efforts, like Sweet Briar College's successful alumni fundraising campaign, which staved off closure. Conversely, Birmingham-Southern College sought county and state funding, but ultimately failed to win that support and closed.[4]

At another level, beyond program and personnel cuts, are institutional mergers. Typically, this involves a larger, financially sound college or university merging with a smaller, troubled one. The usual asymmetry suggests the acquisitions seen in the corporate world, but the merger term remains current in nonprofit higher education. The hope embodied in a merger is that the healthier partner can arrest the other's decline, protecting as many faculty and staff as possible. Students may also benefit by gaining access to more programs and another institution's curriculum.

The reality is that mergers are very complex processes, given the logistical and political challenges of integrating two complicated organisms. Many current and former members of each community may be emotionally invested in maintaining their institution's separate identity. And a campus in financial trouble might not have enough assets to appeal to a would-be merger partner: an attractive academic program or desirable real estate, for example. As with program cuts, there are a good number of merger attempts and successes from recent years to consider. Two California State University campuses combined when one, Cal Maritime, suffered a massive enrollment loss. Conversely, a New England college and university began a merger process, but that fell through when negotiations could not satisfy both sides. Marlboro College shut down as a result, lacking a partner's financial support, while the University of Bridgeport continued on.[5]

A given college or university might consider or attempt mergers and program cuts, only to find its financial straits to still be ruinous. Closing a campus is a deeply fraught, even traumatic experience for the students, faculty, and staff involved. It can damage the reputation and economy of a local community when it loses a neighboring institution. Yet closures have been happening as academia passed its peak. A cluster of for-profit colleges and universities shut down under scrutiny from the Obama administration and amid scandals of poor-quality offerings. Multiple small, private, professionally oriented schools have shuttered themselves, as have some religious institutions. In nearly every case, we have seen enrollment declining, revenue dropping, and costs mounting, often with associated debt.[6]

Closing a college is as complex as merging two or more. An institution has to consider degree completion possibilities for students, the status of internal library colleges and archives, support for faculty and staff finding next jobs or retiring, and the disposition of physical properties, for starters. New positions may appear, such as transition officers; one example is the interim chief restructuring officer organizing the termination of the College of New Rochelle. If a private campus is part of a larger nonprofit, such as a church, there are considerations that follow.

Public institutions have additional legal and political dimensions to work through. Finances need winding up, like endowment gifts whose restrictions must be addressed. A closing college may go through bankruptcy court proceedings. There are so many emotions to address, so many people to support as they go through the process.[7]

If American higher education continues to close, merge, and cut colleges and universities, and does so at a greater level as it proceeds downslope from peak, how might the sector change? The obvious first-order answer is we should expect fewer and/or smaller institutions, overall as the whole ecosystem shrinks to some degree. This would not be a uniform process, as we've said previously, given the scale, relative autonomy, and disaggregated nature of the sector. Elite institutions are better prepared to weather the decline than the rest. Different states and regions are disproportionately affected by various stressors, as demographic and political changes vary throughout the nation. Campuses located in and serving the Northeast and upper Midwest, for example, are more exposed to the K-12 population shrinkage than those in Texas or Florida. The Penn State system closed seven campuses that suffered long-term enrollment decline and had no reasonable chance of an increase. Negative attitudes toward undergraduate education may be more pronounced and have a greater impact in states with persistent Republican legislative majorities than those without. Geography can play another role in terms of local economic viability. A depressed rural or urban area makes it more difficult to attract students (as well as faculty and staff), while a vibrant one can be a boost to recruitment. The broader trend of rural counties seeing their populations age up and shrink, while their economies fall behind urban leaders, adds another challenge to campuses located in the country.[8]

Institutional nature also shapes a given campus's trajectory along the post-peak path. Smaller colleges and universities often have more fragile finances than their larger peers, in part because they cannot realize economies of scale. Private institutions lack the political support of state governments, as we saw very dramatically with the collapse of Birmingham-Southern College, which struggled for years to garner state funding and ultimately failed, then closed. In contrast, a handful of institutions have built enormous student numbers through online learning, such as Arizona State University, Southern New Hampshire University, Western Governors University, and Liberty University. We may see the average or median size of American campuses rise while the total footprint shrinks.[9] [10]

A variation on that online commitment has appeared when a campus downshifts its in-person teaching in favor of distance learning. Such a digital flight can appeal if decision-makers view online as less costly to operate than face-to-face, brick-and-mortar campuses.[11]

Alternatively, the total number of institutions might remain roughly constant, and instead, we see more cuts to programs, faculty, and staff. Mergers and closures are very difficult, as noted, and program cuts usually precede such dire steps. After decades of growth, American higher education has built a substantial edifice. There is a great deal that can be cut before ending a campus. An institution's purpose or identity might shift as a result, such as becoming less liberal arts and more professional, but the entity persists. Particular programs are more likely to face the axe than others, namely the arts and humanities, if current trends continue.[12]

We should bear in mind what happens to campus-adjacent communities as the academic descent continues. Reductions in student populations can have incremental economic and cultural impacts on the local community in terms of fewer customers for businesses, fewer tenants, and fewer workers. They can also change the culture incrementally by reducing the influx of youthful energy typically brought by students of traditional college age. Reductions to academic programs and operational units can have a parallel effect when faculty and/or staff numbers shrink, albeit to different degrees. A campus facing massive cuts, either through its own strategy or through a merger, can depress the community economically and culturally. Businesses that depend on academic clients lose sales, from bookstores to restaurants and apartments. A shuttered campus presents something of a hole in the local social and economic fabric, much as does any failed enterprise with a physical presence in an area.[13]

The federal government can potentially play a role in mitigating or managing this decline. We have some historical precedent for this after the mid-twentieth-century height of state funding. The most ambitious was the 2020 Coronavirus Aid, Relief, and Economic Security (CARES) Act, which poured vast amounts of federal money into the COVID-stricken higher education sector, clearly rescuing programs, people, and institutions from that catastrophe. We could also point to the subsequent Biden administration's efforts to forgive student debt, albeit with mixed results. We could go still further. Author John Warner and others have argued that the federal government should invest in making higher education free to all, much as a mix of governmental funds do the same for primary and secondary schooling. However, the second Trump administration is, as of this writing, pursuing precisely the opposite, cutting a wide range of federal support for higher education, notably research and institutional support grants. For the purposes of this chapter and scenario, we will assume that no such massive policy shift occurs in the near- or medium-term future.[14]

Instead, we can imagine that some local, state, and federal officials may assist campuses in managing the post-peak decline. State governments might assist in helping multiple institutions share some administrative services or curricula. They could facilitate the merging of others into new entities, as when Vermont created Vermont State University (VTSU) out of three campuses: Castleton University, Northern Vermont University, and Vermont Technical College or when the University of Georgia System combined East Georgia State College and Georgia Southern University. When a campus conducts steep cuts or closes, local and state authorities can collaborate to bring relief to the affected communities. This can be challenging politically, of course, as reducing or closing a public college or university can be terrible for a city, county, or state's reputation. Accordingly, we should expect the public sector to sometimes exert itself to maintain its declining postsecondary ecosystem. We might see successful plans appear and become inspirations for other regions.[15]

At the same time, governments may decide not to act and to allow campuses to decline for a range of reasons, including anti-academic ideologies and fierce competition from other causes for scarce resources. One of those reasons is the push to tear up the paper ceiling we noted earlier, a drive to reduce credentialing requirements for public jobs. Recall that such an initiative may stem from progressive politics as well as an anti-academic position. Politicians who want to reduce postsecondary mandates should be less likely to expand efforts to support the institutions that supply them.

We may also see politicians oppose academic measures in favor of supporting alternatives. There is already substantial support for building out America's small apprenticeship system, which can lead its participants from K-12 into employment without spending time in postsecondary education. We may also see political support for boot camps and other competitors to academic experience. Significant political backing for efforts to outflank higher education is likely a feature of the continued post-peak scenario.

President Trump and his supporters are likely to refuse to make public support available in general to higher education. Republican politics have become more opposed to colleges and universities, especially to elite ones and to certain departments (gender and race studies, notably). The major moves we have noted before—cuts to federal research support, ending DEI programs, ending climate change research, terminating trans research and support, intervening in several universities' internal operations, deporting international students, and so on—indicate an attitude that would gladly see at least come campuses decline and fall, and might even push them in that direction. This may become especially evident in states where the GOP controls the legislature and executive, as well as the federal government. In fact, we could consider the Republicans to be the bona fide peak higher education party. If the GOP continues to hold such beliefs as well as to exert power, we may understand it as not just as a supporter of pushing academia further downslope, but as an *accelerant* of post-peak velocity, causing further program cuts, campus closures, and institutional mergers. We've seen one example of this in the attitudes and actions of President Trump and his Department of State against international students, which augur for that population to decline, at least in the short- or medium-term future. In response to these Trumpian actions, some faculty and staff may relocate away from the American academy out of anxiety about Republican policies.

Now that we have sketched out how colleges and universities might respond to a continued peak higher education scenario, we can turn to the three previous chapters exploring higher education as it confronts three immense challenges, seeing how each impacts the sector after its peak.

Artificial intelligence could further drive higher education into decline and challenge academics to respond. An AI industry that the nation perceives as useful and rewarding could cast colleges and universities in a relatively negative light, as expensive, outdated, sclerotic dinosaurs unworthy of support or engagement. Decision-makers thinking in strictly market or transactional terms might assess postsecondary education as losing value and hence worth less support. Funding, both public and private, would generally decline, as would enrollment. Campuses might face growing challenges in recruiting and retaining staff and faculty. The institutional responses we outlined above would become more commonplace, with more cuts, mergers, and closures, further shrinking the entire sector.

Similarly, a public perception that colleges and universities cannot control cheating with AI would further depress institutional value. Employers and society as a whole would consider a biology or history degree to be less impressive than it might have been before ChatGPT and other generative AI systems arrived on the scene, inferring that some or all of the work allegedly completed by the carbon-based graduate was actually done by silicon entities. Stories of students or graduates producing reports and theses with substantial AI contributions may take hold of the national imagination. We can imagine a tide of governmental investigations, academic research, and nonprofit white papers analyzing the extent of the AI-enabled academic dishonesty, criticizing academic offices and practices for not controlling it. We should expect AI cheating to increasingly appear in popular culture, from fiction to songs and nonfiction; digital technology-enabled academic dishonesty has already appeared in literature. That decaying reputation leads to more cuts, mergers, and closures. Colleges and universities would be under pressure to crack down on the problem, incentivized to implement a variety of measures: stricter honor codes, tougher penalties, more intrusive proctoring. Faculty and staff would scramble to offer AI-proof assessments. Vendors would offer a range of support services. Those might drive students away if the students see them as oppressive, intrusive, or dystopian surveillance regimes.[16]

Alternatively, our Collapse 2 scenario envisions AI transforming society in many chaotic and/or negative ways, including making the labor market more challenging and wrecking industries. Campuses could find ways to win more students and general support by positioning themselves as resources for grappling with the crisis, including preparing students for a problematic job market. Rising unemployment and underemployment might send more people to classes, following one historical tendency (albeit one not seen in 2020). Some academics might take up the public intellectual role, bringing their professional expertise to society as a whole, using their deep disciplinary background to help Americans understand and respond to technology-driven disruption.

Yet this might not be a successful strategy for all institutions. Community colleges and some for-profits have the capacity to adapt curricula very quickly toward changes in the labor market, thanks to their respective missions and practices, but not all baccalaureate-granting colleges and research universities have that alignment. Perhaps the latter will struggle more than the former. Moreover, if AI changes the labor market at high speed, academic institutions may struggle to keep up. Some campuses and academics could resist such a career orientation, arguing that higher education classically also has other, non-pecuniary missions: helping students socialize, discover their identities and passions, preparing them for a lifelong love of learning, encouraging them in civic participation, and more. Some professional fields that depend on symbolic analysis and information processing, such as law, journalism, project management, and so on, might see their population shrink, then shift to being more AI-managed. Imagine a 20-person law firm that dwindles to a staff of five, four of whom spend most of their time wrangling software. Not all colleges and universities will be able to prepare their graduates for such a new workplace. If popular perception sees academia as not helping Americans grapple with an AI-transformed society, we might experience further declines in enrollment, engagement, and support, followed by further cuts, mergers, and closures.

Our second large challenge may also drive the peak higher education scenario. Looking ahead for the next decade, we should expect the climate crisis to continue ratcheting up, impacting academia along the lines we described in chapter five: more extreme weather, water quality issues, aridity or drought, flooding, fires, heat waves, and so on, depending on the situation of a given campus and how local Earth systems express global warming. We might see investors or governments disturbed by this process and perhaps unwilling to reduce their carbon emissions, turn instead to conducting major geoengineering efforts. For the latter, it will be interesting to see how many academics support geoengineering for this reason, and how many oppose it for its well-known risks: untested technological implementations; chaotic results of intervening in a massive, complex system; and the responsibility to maintain such a gigantic enterprise lest pausing or ending it cause a termination shock of sudden heating to the earth. Academic engagement with geoengineering could improve our sector's reputation, demonstrating relevance and deep knowledge.[17]

Yet if we expect further climate change developments, with the crisis gradually worsening, the post-peak academic story may deepen. Much depends on the degree to which colleges and universities attain a reputation for addressing global warming through operational transformation, research, and especially teaching. That reputation might consist of both hands-on skills (farming, electrical engineering, conducting therapy for those with climate anxiety or trauma) as well as conceptual knowledge (Earth systems, global macroeconomics, climate sociology). Would-be students, along with potential faculty and staff, may be less inclined to study or work with a campus that does not seem to take the world's greatest crisis seriously. Some may decide to choose their own paths of engagement, such as volunteering, working for a nonprofit or company, or joining a governmental effort. Dread, depression, and resignation over the worsening crisis and its potential future could cause other people to withdraw in despair from study, work, volunteering, or any practical work. As ever, peak can be uneven. Colleges and universities that successfully establish a reputation for climate work could well draw students, faculty, and staff away from competitors that fail to do so.

This is actually a relatively optimistic view of the next two decades. There are marginal possibilities of the crisis becoming much worse, depending again on how multiple Earth systems function. A pause to the Atlantic Meridian Overturning Circulation, a catastrophic collapse of Greenland or Antarctic ice sheets, persistent elevations in temperature or wet bulb temperature could, among other horrors, cause mass migrations away from threatened areas and throw economies into recessions. Damage to the global food system could have similar impacts. Focusing on the significance for American colleges and universities, we can imagine several effects. First, they will have to decide on hosting climate refugees, either in person or for virtual teaching, which modern history indicates can have negative political effects. *Not* supporting migrants might also redound badly. Second, economic downturns impact campus finances. Third, if catastrophes build and Americans consider them urgent, students might prefer to take classes they find more germane to the situation and to avoid others. Funders public and private may withdraw funding from institutions they deem uncommitted to the moment.

Political responses to climate change make the academic situation even more complex. Academics can turn to government funding to conduct climate work, but recent history shows public support can reverse strongly. A local, state, or federal government opposed to climate action can instead challenge academics who do research, teaching, or institutional transformation in that field. Public intellectuals are especially vulnerable to informal and formal pressure and attacks. We might see campus leaders deciding to take what looks like politically safe climate positions, such as saying nothing in public and quietly supporting minimal work at their institutions, especially if they are located in conservative counties and states. Furthermore, to the extent the climate crisis worsens, there is more scope for drastic government action. We can imagine state governments ordering climate refugees off campus grounds, ordering climate classes out of general education, or imposing climate denial academic units. Taken together, the climate situation makes the peak higher education scenario even more challenging.

Divisions over how we respond to climate change and to AI blend into the broader split over how we conceive of the next two hundred years, as we discussed in chapter six. The opposition of what I've called hypermodernists and demodernists may play out in ways that push academia further downslope from peak. To the extent that either ideology becomes influential in a region or state, a campus seen as expressing its opposite may suffer. It's easy to imagine a degrowth-oriented government chastising a business school for too great an advocacy of growth, or a hypermodernist community criticizing a local college for not teaching innovation to a fever pitch. The same would apply to foundations, philanthropic sources, and alumni. Each might look for academic programs, leaders, and entire campuses to support who uphold their views of the best way to carry the human race forward. Given how rapidly we capture and share media, how readily information and reactions race through the world, we may anticipate popular reactions to academics as well, as students share an extended reality (XR) recording terribly hypermodernist class discussion through social media and politicians use reports of demodernist students to argue for defunding state universities.

This great divide might play out at a different, nearly meta level, as adherents to both causes drive attention to great questions of the future and find colleges and universities disinterested in the debate as a whole. After all, campuses play a certain conservative function in preserving the best accumulated knowledge of the human race. Some of our structures are devoted to conservation, such as tenure (protecting some faculty) and funds to preserve a campus's physical plant. To varying degrees, our institutions are ginger about engaging novelty, careful and skeptical about what turns out to be evanescent or irrelevant to our enterprise. Active partisans in the great debate might take their energies elsewhere, to what they see as potentially more productive venues, from politics to popular culture. To the extent we refrain from engaging the debate, academia may lose some relevance, and therefore support, as well as students, faculty, and staff.

As academia continues its managed descent in this scenario, it may acquire a certain momentum. Already, we have seen financial ratings agencies give higher education a negative outlook overall, partly in response to the cuts, mergers, and closures we have discussed. Scholarly problems, including the replication crisis, low citation numbers, AI-enabled scams, predatory journals, and outright fraud, could drain resources and lower scholarship's reputation. In a sense, the worse things look, the worse they might become. Campuses that have outstanding physical plant maintenance, repair, and refurbishment issues will have a harder time taking care of those problems, which will then increase as a result. We may see would-be students, families, cultural figures, analysts, and politicians speaking of higher education as caught in a doom loop, a vicious spiral whereby decline begets further decline. Such discussion and thought then feeds actions, from applications to funding and policies, and so the American academic post-peak doom loop continues.[18]

This would occur unevenly, as we've said throughout this book, depending on variations among institutions, their regions, their strategies, and more. Some of academia's 1%, the elite universities and colleges, will likely maintain their status and wealth, depending on whether the federal government attacks them, while the doom loop damages parts of the rest. The reputation and resource divides currently striating the sector could well deepen. This unevenness might make it harder for campuses to collaborate with each other as they see themselves in a more difficult, even dangerous situation, leading them to take defensive positions. "I've got mine" might describe some institutions' attitudes toward their peers. "Keep our heads down and don't attract attacks" may represent others'. Furthermore, as campuses shrink and close in some regions, postsecondary education deserts might appear.[19]

There will be more wreckage, starting with damaged people, the lives of whom are often missed in the big picture or statistical reports. Impacted faculty and staff will see their careers blocked, sidelined, or ended as their programs or institutions are cut or closed. Students exploring a discipline may find they have to start anew at another campus or in a different program. Communities depending economically and culturally on a vibrant college suffer reductions as that institution shrinks, moves away, or closes. Already, we have seen physical remains of shuttered universities and colleges either being purchased by other entities or left standing, ghost campuses. The further American higher education slides down peak, the more wreckage will result.

Looking further ahead, we can imagine where the vicious cycle might take the postsecondary ecosystem. The whole sector will continue to shrink in terms of enrollment, staffing, physical footprint, financial heft, and reputation until it reaches bottom and stabilizes. Eventually, academia's total capacities come to match social requirements, no longer overbuilt for purpose. In economic terms, supply and demand reach an equilibrium, a vast market correction completed. Perhaps we then see a plateau for some time. Perhaps, if conditions are right, a return to growth occurs. Guiding an institution and its people, doing postsecondary study, teaching students, and conducting research through this downward slope is the task of managed descent.

Taken together, we can now glimpse various ways for American higher education to proceed along the peak higher education path. We can anticipate more program cuts, along with institutional mergers and closures. The postsecondary sector overall appears overbuilt in this future, and as demand for its services declines, a kind of extensive market correction proceeds. This plays out unevenly, of course, with some colleges and universities thriving, especially those that adroitly respond to the crisis, as well as those with high reputations and wealth. Otherwise, we should foresee some mix of fewer programs, academic workers, students, and campuses. Neighboring communities take some hits as a result.

Are there ways for academics to resist this downward slide? What can institutions do to reverse course amid the sector's overall decline and strive for peak once more? Our next chapter will conclude by exploring these options.

CHAPTER 8

Climbing Back to Peak

It is a time of confrontation, this transition, the time of transition of the old society to a new one that does not exist yet, but it's being created with the confrontation of the ghosts.

—PAULO FREIRE

Throughout this book we have developed the peak higher education scenario, putting it through its paces, taking it from the recent past into the next two decades. We have assembled evidence to establish the scenario's plausibility, while also connecting it to many trends and ideas in the higher education ecosystem. We ultimately linked peak academia to some of the largest challenges and ideas facing civilization.

At this point, the reader may experience a sensation all too familiar to futurists. A sense of resignation may have set in. You may feel that American higher education has passed its peak and that continued decline is unlikely to be stopped. It might seem that the forces which drive that dark scenario are too certain, even irresistible, and that nothing can be done to avoid sliding down from it. If so, know that this is a side effect of thinking seriously about the future. We risk losing agency in the face of the depiction of major changes, especially when we back up their description with evidence.

Yet people *do* make the future, including the future of higher education, albeit amid these constraints. It's worth recalling Marx's famous summary, albeit in the gendered language of his time: "Men make their own history, but they do not make it as they please; they do not make it under self-selected circumstances, but under circumstances existing already, given and transmitted from the past." We have agency, in other words, and perhaps a better scope for action, the more we know about those circumstances. In this chapter, we will outline some of the options available to campuses, albeit to different degrees, depending on their distinct circumstances.[1]

I would like to begin by addressing a frequently cited idea in the higher education space. One of the most popular reactions to academic stresses involves asking for a better retelling of the American college and university story. "If only parents/government officials/donors/the media/the public knew the truth about what we do and how we do it," runs the argument, "then they would better support us and stop attacking." Or "We let others, including hostile parties, define us. We should own our own story." If this occurred, then more students would enroll, state governments would increase appropriations and decrease intervening in operations, more donors would fire up their ACH information, and so on. The appeal of better storytelling is clear. Storytelling is, of course, one of the most powerful forms of human communication. For academics who study the humanities, more and better narratives are right in their wheelhouse. There is an element of evidence-based frustration in this idea as well, for anyone in academia who sees themselves or colleagues doing important and effective work, yet finds the broader world failing to attend to it. In response, it seems reasonable for post-peak academics to call for more and better storytelling about our work and world.

Objections to this call do not appear as often, but I would like to rehearse them here, because I find the idea frustrating. One rejoinder is that American colleges and universities *already* invest heavily in storytelling. We retain a number of lobbyists at both state and federal levels whose entire job is to convey these narratives to decision makers, and who have done so for decades. An entire industry is built around spreading the good work of campuses, as campus communication, public relations specialists, admission offices, and advancement departments (sometimes slammed as part of "administrative bloat") energetically find and make media to share, carefully calibrating dissemination to various audiences and venues, from advertisements and web pages to Tiktok videos and various forms of viewbooks, not to mention protocols for managing faculty, staff, and student expressions. Multiple third-party vendors assist in this work, including consultants and technology providers. Administrations select architects and campus planners to produce the most appealing spatial experience for visitors. Additionally, some faculty and staff conduct public intellectual work, sharing their professional expertise with the broader public, carrying with it the additional message that academics perform interesting, important, and high-quality research and teaching. A swarm of reporters covers higher education, some in a very supportive way. Beyond that, we have had the cultural consensus described in chapter three singing the praises of higher education, telling the story of its necessity, for decades, including to young children and often by authority figures. All of this storytelling, this small academic narrative industry, is, apparently, falling short and needs revision. If that is correct, it should count as one of the most colossal storytelling failures in modern history. It seems also to be a scandal implicating a significant number of people, including a number of academic professionals. This would entail a reckoning and massive reorganization, neither of which seems to be in the offing as of this writing.

As someone who has researched and taught storytelling for decades, I find the better storytelling cry unsatisfactory for a very simple reason. There is no organization of the higher education story at scale. While campus communication offices borrow from each other, they strive to make their institution stand out against other institutions in a steadily increasing competition. Lobbyists work through a variety of rhetorical and political situations, hitting different notes and themes as needed. Academic public intellectuals work from their individual perspectives, and so on. Given the sheer diversity of story actions and styles in play, it seems unlikely that *all* are failing, yet that is what the call for better academic storytelling entails.

This is not to deny the effect of multiple anti-academic narratives in play. Pro-academic stories have underpinned the long growth period higher education enjoyed until the early 2020s (described in our earlier chapters), but countervailing stories have already been in the air. They have roots reaching far back in American culture and history. Charges that higher education indoctrinates young minds into DEI support, transgenderism, cultural Marxism, censorship, and antisemitism build on previous complaints about political correctness, feminism, and antimilitarism, not to mention older criticisms of teaching anti-Americanism, racial insurgency, and straight-up Marxist revolution. Today, a large ecosystem circulates the new-ish narratives through conservative sources across multiple media (podcasts, social media, Fox News, Truth Social) and into the mainstream through various openings. Academics and our supporters can and do counter these stories, some of us in public and at some risk to ourselves.

We can always improve stories, especially ones for large, diverse audiences, over time. But perhaps a better idea at this point is not to rest academia's post-peak hopes on refining the story told about us, but to change and improve *what the story describes*. This is not a question of representation so much as what is represented. We should consider how to improve and redesign colleges and universities so that honest stories reflect evident improvement. To paraphrase Ernest Rutherford and Henry Tizard, we are out of money, so we will have to rethink what we do. Then the better stories may follow.

Returning Enrollment

Since the peak higher education scenario rests centrally on enrollment, we can start with ways to attempt to grow student numbers. Some of these are well-known and already practiced. At the global level, recruiting more international students is a modern classic, as students from other countries tend to have higher socioeconomic status and therefore contribute to a campus's bottom line. Institutions committed to some degree of global education find foreign students a good fit on that score. Additionally, they may contribute to diversity goals if they represent a non-write race or ethnicity. Since the end of the Cold War, American colleges and universities have accordingly pursued international students. There are organizations and businesses that support such efforts. Indeed, a meta-association recently launched to increase international student numbers, the US for Success Coalition (USSC), intended to "expand the destinations for international students to include a broader range of higher education institutions, including community colleges, historically black colleges and universities, and other minority-serving institutions."[2]

This strategy continues to appeal but has run into challenges. One recent development in its favor has been several nations, formerly very attractive to global students, strongly cutting back on their numbers. Australia, Britain, and especially Canada have competed with the United States on this front, but each saw their enrollment fall, creating a broader market for American colleges and universities. Additionally, some nations and regions, notably the sub-Saharan area, have yet to process through the demographic transition and so will continue to provide traditional-age undergraduate populations in high numbers. However, popular American anti-immigrant sentiment rose sharply over the past decade, commensurate with candidate and President Trump's views, which can dissuade some would-be students from applying to such an unfriendly country. Stories of violence, such as school and mass shootings, circulate widely, portraying a dangerous nation with unsafe educational environments. In other words, while campuses may seek to boost international enrollment to reduce post-peak problems, such a strategy may be difficult to implement.[3]

Another distant recruiting option that is closer to home is the classic habit of a state university enrolling students from other states, charging much higher tuition. Nothing in the physical world justifies this differential—for example, students from one state away do not pay less than students from the other side of the continent—but the political factor of crossing a state boundary so far justifies price hikes. State governments can impose limits on this practice, arguing that a state university should serve its own population first and foremost. Yet the ability to bring in more revenue, combined with the attraction of an interstate reputation, can persuade legislatures to welcome out-of-staters at scale. When Madison removed their out-of-state cap, that group's enrollment soared by nearly one-third. An extreme example is the University of Vermont, where fewer than one-quarter of its students came from the Green Mountains. It seems likely that this option will remain on the table where governments choose not to rein it in.[4]

Another option for growing enrollment is to expand online teaching. Distance learning offers the chance to expand student numbers through its convenience, with students not having to physically commute to a campus or reside there. Offering online classes does not require building out additional classrooms, student unions, or residence halls. It also provides the learner with a greater set of campus options, as one can potentially take classes anywhere in the world. On top of this is the little-appreciated fact that we now have decades of online pedagogical practice to build from, amply documented and analyzed in scholarship. There is also a growing body of professionals in fields like educational technology, learning design, and educational development who can assist online class creation and refinement.

However, entering online learning at scale or expanding one's offerings presents major challenges. Successful remote instruction requires a complex series of activities and infrastructure, from a technological substrate (sufficient hardware, software, bandwidth) to redesigned classes, selecting and redeveloping a curriculum, faculty and staff development, multiple enterprise systems, a cybersecurity strategy, a new enrollment approach, and more. This is one reason online program management (OPM) firms have grown, albeit to uneven levels of performance and fees. Furthermore, any college or university starting in this field in the 2020s will find it already occupied by established competitors, especially the mega universities teaching enormous numbers of students at scale, from Western Governors and Arizona State University to Southern New Hampshire University. Campuses need time to build up the human experience of teaching well online, which requires a mix of hiring, professional development, support, and nurturing communities of practice. Further, an institutional drive to expand online education can meet resistance from faculty and alumni who view remote learning as subpar or too removed from their particular institutional mission.[5]

Another strategy for boosting student numbers has proven very successful in the past several years. Community colleges use dual enrollment offers to recruit high school students to take classes at their institutions. This has significantly increased their class numbers. Indeed, dual enrollment seems to be the major drive behind the 2024 enrollment rebound. The appeal of such classes is evident, as they offer expanded curricular experiences for high school students while using preexisting community college capacity (classrooms, instructors, support staff). Community colleges' deep attunement to community needs makes them quite able to configure class offerings for local demand. It is an open question as to the ability of other institutions to take advantage of this practice.[6]

On that inter-institutional theme, improved credit transfer may also increase student enrollment and even completion. Roughly one-third of postsecondary students transfer between institutions, according to a 2017 federal report. Many students find difficulties in translating credits from one institution to another, a process that is often opaque (especially to first-generation learners) and frustrating, especially as one sees one's academic achievements downgraded. That federal report found that students lost 43% of their credits through transfer, losing nearly one-half of their academic work. Additionally, the process can take a great deal of time. Such difficulties can slow or block student progress. There are many ideas and practices available for improving academic credit mobility, including building up articulation agreements between individual campuses, enhancing credit transfer across institutions in the same or related public systems, building or improving existing digital transfer systems, and making the entire system more transparent. Improving academic advising can have a positive impact. Some states, such as Idaho, have seen campuses adopt common course numbering systems, at least for general education.

There is also the practice of reverse transfer, whereby a four-year institution awards an associate's degree to a student transferring from a community college in recognition of their work. As Charles M. Ambrose and Michael T. Nietzel make the case for reverse transfer:

> Each year thousands of community college students transfer to four-year colleges without having finished their AA. Many of these students ultimately drop out of college, exiting, despite years of study and a mountain of debt, without any formal higher education credential to their credit. Reverse transfer changes that equation. Instead of going 0 for 2 in the degree column, students can "reach back" and earn an associate of arts degree, and those who persist can add a BA to the final ledger. This recover-your-degree strategy can be a focus of an outreach by colleges that are intent on increasing enrollment by transfer students.[7]

Colleges and universities can also strive to recruit more students by aligning curricula with major social causes, sometimes in response to social changes. Cybersecurity coursework and programs have become increasingly popular due to the world's strong demand for protection against digital threats. Indeed, several program leaders have told me they have a difficult time graduating students, as governments and businesses hire students out of their programs before they even complete their degrees. Social justice courses and programs have had a similar appeal, especially following the 2020 murder of George Floyd and the national turn toward antiracist activism. Along similar lines, climate change study has the potential to attract students, especially traditional-age undergraduates who tend to be more invested in global warming than their elders, as I have previously argued.

The state-level gradual decriminalization of some drug laws and criminal enforcement has led some campuses to offer more study options for cannabis and psychedelics, depending on local conditions. For example, in 2024, the University of Colorado Denver opened its Center for

Psychedelic Research, directed by a professor of psychology. The University of Maryland now offers a Master of Science in Medical Cannabis Science and Therapeutics as well as a graduate certificate in Medical Cannabis Science, Therapeutics, and Policy; Roanoke College makes available a Bachelor of Science in Cannabis Science, a BS in Cannabis Social Justice & Policy, and a minor in Cannabis Studies. Each class and program has the possibility of engaging students in newly available or rapidly growing fields. Yet each of these approaches risks backfiring when social conditions change. For example, the second Trump administration's hostility to climate action may cause some campus leaders to back away from academic programs anchored on global warming. Similarly, the government's opposition to DEI may have a comparable effect on social justice studies.[8]

Beyond changing what we teach, higher education can also shift who we recruit. The classic stereotype of undergraduate education features an 18-to-22-year-old student, and that population does, of course, exist and represent a majority, although published data on this score varies. In 2021, 85% of college students were 25 years old and younger, according to one federal report, although institutional types saw clear differences: "Ninety-one percent of full-time undergraduate students at public 4-year institutions were under the age of 25, compared with 87 percent at private nonprofit 4-year institutions and 79 percent at public 2-year institutions." Other federal reports put the over-25 proportion at 32% in 2023. The Lumina Foundation claims 34% of students are 25 and older. We can see the general pattern beneath these variations of some minority of students being adults, while the traditional pupil is a later teenager/person in their early twenties. This tradition will be under increasing pressure due to the demographic transition we described in our earlier chapters, as childbirth numbers decline, accentuated by the Great Recession's demographic cliff and the potential for immigration to drop due to political reasons.[9]

One strategic response available to colleges and universities is to recruit more adults, even to make adult learners the new traditionals. For some institutions, this has long been the practice. Some state universities and most community colleges have enrolled many adults for years. One analysis showed 43% of community college students aged over 25 in the mid-2010s, while another found the average age of such a student to be 28 at that time. They can respond to the demographic transition by doubling down on that practice. In contrast, campuses that largely serve traditional-age students, such as liberal arts colleges and flagship public universities, have the opportunity to shift classes by recruiting more adults—and, in so doing, learn from their other state and community institutional peers. They can reach out to adults seeking to supercharge their present careers or switch to another. They can also engage the adults who pursued the skilled trades early in life and now wish to return to academics, perhaps for health reasons. Additionally, Sarah Damaske and Adrianne Frech have identified a good number of men for whom adult employment has been precarious and uneven, for whom a college degree might be a useful benefit. There may be a social justice implication to recruiting more adults, as campuses can reach out to populations underrepresented in the traditional-age population. There is especially the large number of people who took some postsecondary classes but never completed a degree program, the Some College, No Credential (SCNC) population, a total the National Student Clearinghouse estimated at 36.8 million in 2022. These can be challenging groups to recruit, however. SCNC people may feel angry at college experiences and are unlikely to want to return to them—especially if they have spent years wrestling with paying loans for that experience. Institutions historically focused on welcoming teenagers may not be so welcoming for middle-aged men and women.[10]

Colleges and universities could go further along this line of recruiting adults by reaching out to senior citizens. That population is likely to continue growing as part of the demographic transition, unless we suffer more pandemics like COVID-19, which tend to kill many elders. At present, senior citizens have several roles in higher education, besides working as faculty and staff, depending on retirement practices. In some states, seniors already receive preferential pricing at steep discounts for postsecondary credits from public universities. A number of colleges and universities support instances of the Osher Lifelong Learning Institute, focused on teaching elders. Private institutions like Rollins College offer or have offered a range of programs dedicated to senior citizens. Arizona State University built on-campus senior housing. Looking forward, we could imagine more such offerings aimed at recruiting our growing over-65 population.

Taking lifelong learning seriously remains a viable strategy for a good number of institutions seeking to avoid continuing to slide down from peak higher education. Depending on its nature, a campus could reach out to alumni in multiple ways. It could use distance learning technologies to reconnect graduates with beloved faculty members or to welcome them virtually to exciting campus events. A successful educational experience might attract an alumnus to revisit the institution for subsequent schooling. The college or university one had a positive experience with at an early point in life might become a trusted partner for many needs throughout life. A Stanford University project coined the term "Open Loop" to describe learners returning to higher education at many points, or "episodes," in their lives. One might start as an undergraduate, receive a degree, enter the workforce for a decade, then take classes again to upskill or change careers. Another might revisit campus to finally realize a lifelong interest. If we think more broadly, perhaps turning to the grand challenges we discussed in chapters four through six, those whose careers or whole lives have been thrown askew by climate change, AI, and/or the general civilizational polycrisis may well decide they need more postsecondary experience to thrive, survive, or just cope. Much of this strategy depends on a college or university deliberately and carefully nurturing these alumni relationships, especially online.[11]

Campuses have still other options for trying to return to peak. The financial system by which we maintain institutional operations remains problematic, as we discussed earlier in this volume, so rethinking higher education economics is certainly an area of inquiry and experimentation. Changing published price and charging systems offers one way to improve an institution's reputation—for example, by cutting the posted tuition and fees—to appeal to students and families worried about inflation. This can be risky if it yields a net revenue reduction. State-funded tuition programs can even appeal more strongly to would-be pupils. There is a wide range of these, from free tuition plus some fees for certain campuses (often community colleges) to "last mile" schemes (paying what families cannot) to free tuition for students working in fields the state values. Boosting published prices might seem counterintuitive, but that might appeal to wealthy families seeking a sense of exclusivity and luxury.[12]

Another administrative strategy for attracting more students is direct admission. This describes when a college or university proactively accepts certain students *without them applying*. The campus identifies promising students and grants them admission. One study found Idaho universities increased enrollment for some students, such as first-generation ones, but did not adjust applications from underrepresented populations. Augsburg University had a similar experience, yet managed to increase the latter. A related strategy to direct admissions is guaranteeing admissions to students who meet certain criteria. For example, in 2023, Virginia Commonwealth University offered such acceptance to high school seniors "who are among the top 10% of their high school graduating class or have a high school GPA of 3.5 or above." In a sense, these plans are based on simplifying the complex American admissions process, or taking the anxiety out of it.[13]

On the opposite end of the spectrum of making it easier for students to apply is the policy of reducing or ending legacy admissions, which is the established habit of giving preference to the children of an institution's alumni. The preference can be quite significant, as when Harvard University's legacy admission acceptance rate of 33% dwarfed its general rate of just over 3%. Institutions justify the practice because it brings a family into a closer relationship with the college or university, and also is likely to improve alumni giving, but critics charge that this disproportionately rewards wealthy families. Moving against legacy admissions can be a way for a campus to diversify its student body, while also appealing to progressive applicants and their families. A series of private colleges and universities have publicly reduced or terminated the practice. One state government outlawed it for its private campuses.[14]

From Quantity to Quality

Now we can discuss another way of attempting to return higher education to peak, that of improving the student experience. This is, of course, a huge topic and one as old as universities, as we have long sought to better the academic enterprise. There is a library of books on the subject stuffed with strategies and schools of thought. Here we can draw attention to a set of ideas which are currently in play and might extend across American academia, with a focus on how such practices might help attract and retain students to try to reverse the post-peak slide.

We can start by pointing to various forms of active learning, which, following a constructivist framework, have students do more than watch an instructor and take notes on the experience. Instead, students conduct experiments and do field work outside the typical classroom, for example. Within the classroom, we know of and practice many forms of small group work and peer instruction, from think-pair-share exercises to using clickers to foment discussion. Socratic questioning, active seminar discussions, and energetic labs are also long-standing active learning techniques, if underappreciated as such; the flipped classroom is, in a sense, a more recent iteration of these. Multiple studies have shown implementations that improve students' test results and grades, not to mention self-reported satisfaction, as well as aiding underrepresented students. Some universities are supporting active learning strategically.[15]

We can also consider the modern science of learning, a body of knowledge that has used neuroscience and cognitive science to understand how humans best expand their understanding. Summarizing that field of research and practice is beyond the scope of this chapter. For now, we can point to its existence and many practical benefits for individual instructors, as well as the possibilities for a campus to support it strategically.[16]

That strategic question is one worth noting. A great deal of teaching development occurs at the level of an individual faculty member seeking to improve their practice. Institutions can commit to supporting their entire instructional workforce in this effort. Historically, professional development funding, peer efforts, and hosting local workshops have been ways to accomplish this. As noted above, professional staff capacities have grown in the twenty-first century in the forms of educational technology, educational development, and instructional design. Calls for taking the scholarship of teaching seriously in terms of faculty hiring, promotion, and tenure persist. Teaching and learning centers, along with associated paracurricular units such as quantitative reasoning groups and GIS labs, also represent ways by which a college or university can support pedagogical improvement at an institutional scale.[17]

Campuses can also work to improve their use of educational technology. This is, once more, a field already broad enough to have its own library of books, not to mention competing schools of thought, established major problems, and multiple traditions of practice, and thus beyond the scope of this chapter to decently summarize. We can point to several key points in the context of using educational technology to help colleges and universities improve the learner's experience. First, as the number of students taking classes entirely online grows, it is incumbent upon us to make that experience excellent, which means revising and rethinking instruction in that mode. The negative cases of COVID-19-era emergency instruction can be useful in this regard. Second, we can explore more innovative ways of incorporating ed tech within the curriculum, from the digital liberal arts to the digital humanities. There is an ed tech tradition of students actively using computing to produce learning in the constructivist tradition; others, such as Stephen Downes, have called for a "connectivist" form of teaching and learning using the social affordances of digital networks. Third, we can also explore new forms of inter-institutional classes which combine online and in-person learning. The experiment with teaching upper-level humanities seminars across multi-campus consortia organized by the Council of Independent Colleges offers one fruitful example. I myself have piloted such classes, such as a multi-campus seminar on the American war in Vietnam with colleagues from other colleges and universities. Fourth, we can recall the great tradition of using digital technologies specifically to spur learning and creativity dating back to the foundational work of Alan Kay and Seymour Papert. Fifth, we can explore and use the possibilities of emerging technologies for learning and research, such as XR.[18]

Institutions can also pilot certification options other than the received ones. Competency-based learning can speed a student's course through a curriculum, reducing their time to degree, reducing their expenses, and also, sometimes, giving them the opportunity to explore further studies. Certificates can appeal to learners who prefer an even shorter course of study, giving them tangible academic recognition. Some educators may lament reduced time in the postsecondary space, but a full four years of undergraduate experience (more often five or more) does not suit every adult's life situation. Indeed, student interest in certificates appears to be rising, as expressed by the number of certificates awarded.[19]

More ambitiously, academics may rethink certification in a radical way. Currently, most certification is done in-house, as campuses award recognition through degrees, built on smaller identifications through grades. Perhaps we could outsource these forms of achievement designation. This might sound surprising, but consider the extent to which a given department or campus already does related forms of this through accreditation (conducted by agencies and peers) and professional recognition (professional organization or business exams). We could design systems whereby a student must pass a rigorous assessment offered by qualified representatives of another academic institution or association. In this way, we determine academic achievement in a broader context, beyond immediate interpersonal relationships, to a heightened professional level. As cultural shifts and AI raise questions about academic quality, perhaps rethinking our certification systems will amplify our rigor objectively and in terms of popular perception.[20]

In fact, our institutions can focus even more closely on student lives by doubling down on questions of equity and identities. Some campuses and programs have done so historically, at times in response to social movements (the 1950s and 1960s civil rights movement) and also motivated by internal developments (the 1980s push for more students of color, ultimately caricatured as "political correctness"). In our time the resurgence of antiracist activism following the 2020 George Floyd murder drove a wave of actions across higher education, from changing the physical campus (statues, building names) to rethinking faculty and staff representation through hiring and professional support, redesigning the curriculum to be more culturally responsive, launching efforts to redress historical wrongs (i.e., Georgetown University's The Descendants Truth & Reconciliation Foundation), and offering antiracist education for the whole community. For several years, there was a great deal of financial and institutional investment, some trial and error, a good amount of learning, all buttressed by a growing body of scholarship. There are many interventions to make and many ways to assess progress. In short, we can better serve students from underrepresented racial backgrounds.[21]

We can improve the student experience through gender identity as well. Decades of work have sought to improve women's postsecondary studies and have resulted in a great deal of success, perhaps most notably in the fact that women have outnumbered men as students for years, as we discussed earlier. Much work remains, of course, such as in matching male and female compensation for the same work, advancing women in male-dominated disciplines, and boosting the number of women in institutional leadership positions. We can advance further along this path and likely improve the experience of female students in our colleges and universities. At the same time, we can improve men's experience, especially as (as we also noted earlier) significant numbers of boys and men avoid considering postsecondary education. This is fraught territory politically and culturally, but an academic institution dedicated to caring for its students should surely be able to use its creative powers and ethos of service to enhance how we treat all genders. This also means supporting well people who exist outside the traditional gender binary, such as nonbinary and trans individuals.[22]

Obviously, such focused care for students based on their gender or race runs directly into political opposition, and as of this writing, there is no good solution. Such opposition grew after 2020 and attained national preeminence with the installation of a second Trump administration, backed up by Republican majorities in Congress and conservative support on the Supreme Court. Doing race and gender work has never been easy, but it is much more challenging in this environment, as of this writing. Advocates have been scrambling and getting creative in trying to conduct the work by changing keywords ("belonging" instead of "DEI"), distributing functions to less controversial units (student life, mental health counseling, faculty development), relying on local or state governmental support where it exists, and more. It is an open question how far gender and race progress can go in this environment, and to what extent politics whittles it down. We do know that if institutions can commit to such support, we can improve the experiences—and the lives—of students.

Another institutional strategy to support students by identity is to dedicate a campus to serving one population as a strategic focus. Historically Black colleges and universities can create a shared community space for Black students. Students who feel uncomfortable or actively opposed as minorities in a majority-serving institution may have better experiences in HBCUs. Latino students may prefer campuses that serve substantial numbers of their peers, Hispanic-serving institutions (HSIs) being the federally recognized category. Similarly, women's colleges may become more sought after.[23]

The range of activities just mentioned points to another, more generalized strategy of improving academic quality, that of wraparound support. American higher education already has a globally unusual amount of student care. While many universities around the world focus on offering classes and research, the United States presents students with an additional, full range of other activities and services, from mental health support to athletics, physical safety measures, food pantries, family housing, study abroad opportunities, internships, interest groups and clubs to multitudinous cocurricular activities. Colleges and universities can double down on this, improving those services and offering newer ones, such as esports leagues, help with political organizing, and more technological options. We can offer a richer experience to students when they join us, hopefully becoming more attractive in the process.

A related call for improving academic quality comes from the Paradigm Project, a Bringing Theory to Practice initiative and with which, in full disclosure, I work on one committee. The Paradigm Project calls for bringing academic creativity to bear on reinventing education at scale, systematically, not piecemeal. A key part of that reform involves colleges and universities serving the whole student, across multiple domains. In the words of the project's founder, David Scobey, "Students deserve an education in which—as in their actual lives—economic needs and goals are inseparable from personal, family, community, civic, and even spiritual needs and goals." Scobey envisions a campus that teaches students through experiential, classroom, and service learning combined. Such an institution would honor and incorporate student voice and agency. All of this would be done with a focus on equity and social justice.[24]

All of these approaches may potentially attract more students to our campuses, to apply, to learn, to complete degrees, but we don't have to do them in isolation. Inter-institutional collaboration remains an area with much underutilized potential. Colleges and universities can share "backend" resources, such as data storage, learning management systems, library collection storage and provision, emergency planning, and even some financial operations, realizing cost savings along the way. A group of six New York liberal arts institutions (also known as The New York 6) pooled resources across that state to reduce medical costs, to share a cybersecurity office each could not have well afforded individually, and to reduce some purchases through shared procurement practices. These are not services that greet would-be students as offerings unique to a given institution, nor is their branding as such very productive. They do not stand out in the popular imagination when we think of college, but they can save money.

Yet "front-end" collaborations between campuses can also benefit. Low-hanging fruit here is when institutions, their units, or even individual professionals share their experiences and reflections with others. This often happens informally, both through traditional means (conferences, meetings, personal communications, publications on pedagogy and academic administration) and digital ones (social media, video, podcasts, etc.). Some formal mechanisms exist for this, from professional bodies' meetings and communications to academic research and publication. One dedicated example of this is the Bringing Theory to Practice collaborative's Changemakers Network, which brings together academics exploring and implementing progressive institutional reform. Individual campuses can share courses with each other, broadening their curricular offerings while connecting students with new peers. This is especially beneficial for institutions lacking the scope and resources to offer a full university's worth of class topics. One consortium of small colleges realized an additional benefit by making upper-level humanities courses available to the group, giving passionate faculty a better chance of teaching their beloved topics to a bigger audience, as noted earlier. Beyond peer partnerships, campuses can partner with what James Shulman describes as "synthetic organizations," entities that broker service provision to lower costs. The scholarly publication provider JSTOR offers an example of this, digitizing, organizing, and making available a massive research archive which no one institution could reasonably have done on its own. The digital image archive Artstor plays a similar role in making available high-quality visuals for art classes as well as across the curriculum. At best, such partnerships can improve a college or university's quality of offerings, save money, or both.[25]

Conversely, and perhaps more likely, institutions would decide to outcompete others more fiercely. American higher education is already and has long been quite competitive for multiple reasons, including the way that leadership teams often receive more incentives to compete than to collaborate. The forces we have outlined in the preceding chapter will make campuses keener to attract students and resources from others. That drive can elicit creative institutional responses, which might improve students' experiences, as well as perhaps improve the lives of those who work there. Such competition could have negative effects as well on an individual campus, including, for example, cutting staff compensation or student life services in order to reduce costs. At a macro level, we might not see net gains if some college successes weaken other institutions, winning students while depressing enrollment elsewhere.

Increased competition in the post-peak era might see different groups of academic institutions turn against each other, or benefit from another's losses. We are already accustomed to public universities competing with those in other states for often higher out-of-state tuition. We may see public flagship universities and those with famous sports teams increasingly attracting students from other campuses in their systems. Smaller institutions, such as small liberal arts colleges, might be able to adapt to change and pivot to new structures more quickly than their more massive competitors. Private and public colleges and universities already compete, each using their unique advantages (state support, private autonomy). Perhaps community colleges will thrive against all others, as they have already made significant enrollment headway through dual enrollment programs that allow high school students to take college courses for credit. Some are pushing local and state governments for the ability to grant bachelor's degrees, directly competing with baccalaureate-offering colleges and universities. Their intensive connections to local business needs position them well for would-be students focused on postsecondary education for labor market benefits. Their combination of low price points with community immersion remains appealing. They also tend to evade charges of political bias, which mostly adhere to elite colleges and universities. Meanwhile, all campuses can compete for private funding.

With these strategies and options in mind—and they are by no means an exhaustive list—we can consider how colleges and universities might respond positively to the three great challenges we explored in chapters four through six. How can those responses help propel colleges and universities back up toward peak?

A campus engaging deeply with AI might position itself to attract more students. If the college embeds AI within its curriculum and pedagogy to an extent that potential students can perceive and appreciate, and if enough such would-be learners apply and actually attend, then a pro-AI strategy might yield an enrollment boost. More visible AI research might have a similar effect, such as a professor winning attention for an influential book or article. Similarly, a perception that a university is using AI in its operations in appealing ways might also gain attention and applications. What might heighten these impressions is the sense that they improve the academic experience and/or reduce student costs.

Note the conditionals in the preceding paragraph. If, if, if—we can easily imagine ways such an approach could fail. A campus might invest resources into an AI-forward plan, with a great deal of activity by staff and faculty, but all of that work does not manage to register in the outside world. Alternatively, such an effort might backfire if would-be pupils assess it to produce a degraded or inferior experience, such as fearing software would replace humans in an unpleasant way or that a school overinvested in tech and underinvested in student amenities. A third way for AI to backfire would be if the potential student body becomes opposed to the technology in general, and hence would be appalled by a campus saturated in it. In fact, as we noted previously, one strategy for a campus would be a retro one, deliberately refusing AI in an attempt to appeal to similarly minded learners.

Along similar lines, a college or university may commit itself to climate action, hoping to win more students who find that to be a high value. To review, this can be done at several levels. First, offering an expansive learning experience concerning global warming could occur through classes across the curriculum and supportive pedagogy. Second, various certifications can recognize climate study, including certificates, micro-credentials, undergraduate, and graduate degrees. Third, research conducted by faculty (as well as staff and students) can grow with departmental and dean-level support. Fourth, a campus could change its operations and physical plant to mitigate or adapt to climate change, from buildings and energy use to food service and campus grounds. Fifth, an institution can engage in the world beyond campus boundaries through community partnerships and public intellectual work. Sixth, an academic community can deeply rethink what it means to be a learning enterprise in light of this civilization's crisis. Taken together, we can imagine a climate campus, or a university dedicated to the new liberal arts of grappling with global warming. This might appeal to younger would-be students who tend to be more engaged with the topic than their elders. It might appeal to a larger audience as the crisis deepens.

As with AI, we can see ways in which such a climate strategy might fail. It would not appeal to students for whom climate change is not a major concern, or who deny its existence and importance. A campus climate effort might occur but not succeed in communicating itself to the world. A negative political response at local, state, or national levels (or all three) could generate enough bad reputation to swamp any enrollment growth, while also causing multiple forms of institutional grief. Committing to serious climate engagement entails risk, as well as an expectation of rising global warming interest from the academic community and the world of potential students.

Likewise, colleges and universities face a strategic choice when they consider engaging with the great ideological divide we outlined in chapter six. We can imagine a campus committing to the hypermodern vision, energetically supporting research, especially into the hard sciences and growth-oriented innovation. It would expand its physical footprint and student body quantitatively and qualitatively, always seeking to improve its buildings and services. Hypermodern University would transfer knowledge to the world and the immediate community in the spirit of accelerating civilizational development. Its ambitions would run high, seeking to create an ever-advancing world and to prepare students for it.

Conversely, a demodernist campus would prepare for a world that no longer grows, or sees humanity's footprint receding. Its physical and infrastructural footprint gradually shrinks, taking up less space and hosting a smaller population. Demodernist University would reach this great transformation across the disciplines, as the natural sciences, the humanities, the social sciences, and the arts consider how humanity suspends its long habit of growth. Its classes would prepare students for this world, especially helping them enter a very new world of work and different politics. Perhaps these academics urge their population and the world to deliberately choose to step back from hypermodernity as the best and most ethical choice, or instead argue that demodernity is inevitable and academia's role is to see humanity into it in as humane a way as possible.

Committing a campus to any of these strategies—hypermodernism, demodernism, climate action, pro- or anti-AI—constitutes a bet on the future. A given campus would have to conduct careful research, institutional reflection, open conversations with its full community, and thoughtful strategic planning to see if any one would be worth pursuing for their given situation and identity. Each offers a possible route back toward peak higher education.

To conclude: We can view the recent history of American higher education as one wherein the sector overshot its peak. We had grown and developed colleges and universities to their greatest height, building on a history of steady enrollment and financial growth, then found it all overbuilt for its purpose once demand began to slacken. This is one way of understanding the pain and friction academia now experiences. We are suffering from excess capacity.

If those conditions persist, *if* demand continues to stay below circa 2012 levels, we should expect more expressions of post-peak institutional contraction, as noted in chapter seven. Campuses will seek new revenue forms, lease or sell off properties, reduce services, cut programs, cut staff and faculty, merge, or close. Overbuilt for its needs, the sector will continue to contract. The late-twentieth-century belief in "college for all" will dwindle into "college for some" or perhaps back to the older practice of "college for a few." Academia's reputation will suffer overall. There will be more human suffering through this process as the post-peak situation disrupts courses of study and professionals' careers. The amount of human improvement through education, research, and public service will decline.

We also confront that vision under a dreadful amount of political pressure. The second Trump administration and its very supportive Republican Party have waged an aggressive campaign against the postsecondary sector, from cutting federal research funding to taking out university presidents, intervening in institutional autonomy, and launching multiple investigations. Some state governments have acted along similar lines, increasing control of university operations, trying to end progressive DEI and gender policies, altering the accreditation landscape for partisan ends, and more. Many of the academics I've spoken with over the past year—professors, students, librarians, provosts, grants officers, presidents, technologists, residence life directors, food service providers, scholarly publishers, foundation officers, state politicians, federal officials, among others—have described feeling terrified for their institutions, their professions, their careers, even their families. As of this writing, there has been some activity aimed at protecting academia from these attacks, with several presidents speaking up, some staff and faculty making public their thoughts, and some academic participation in broader political activities, such as protests and local campaigns. A small number of academics have opposed them, expressing support for various Republican policies. And what looks like a much larger academic population has fallen silent. Keeping one's head down, avoiding taking a stand, focusing on doing as much of one's work as possible without drawing fire—this seems to be an emergent strategy. Perhaps Trump will succeed in damaging higher education, taking the whole sector down some notches, strewing institutional and human wreckage.

Yet none of this is certain, not our political responses to one administration nor our strategic actions in the face of longer-running trends. Continued post-peak American academia is one scenario of many possible futures. Student demand might return to some higher level than now, perhaps reaching a plateau. Individual campuses and academics can turn their immense intellectual capacities, creativity, and passion for the work into creating new institutional forms and practices, better supporting students, continuing to produce world-leading research, and serving communities. In other words, the threat posed by having passed peak might elicit a positive, countervailing renaissance for American higher education. As part of that potential positive turn, academics grappling with the world's largest problems may give us additional pathways forward.

To return to an earlier theme, there is another sense of "peak" beyond the statistical rise and fall curve. We also speak of peak as a positive height to aspire to, as in peak performance and peak experience, the personal acme of achievement and intensity, attained after thoughtful and sustained work. This chapter's title, returning to peak, seeks to evoke that sense of literally extraordinary performance. When an academic institution seeks to reach peak, it can do so in the *quantitative* sense of increasing enrollment and other metrics, but may also strive for that *qualitative* upward leap in what we do and how we do it. Perhaps after decades of massified higher education, when we successfully grew higher education in terms of quantity, our next era will be a qualitative one.

Academics occupy an unusual and, I think, beautiful position in American society, with our triple mission of teaching, research, and service. We nurture creativity and preserve the record of human intellectual achievement. We work to high standards of human support and social contribution. We contribute to humanity's understanding of the world's greatest challenges. Faced with post-peak higher education, we now have the opportunity to rethink and redesign our enterprise and to work toward a new peak. May we do so with care.

NOTES

Epigraphs

Jorge Coronado, Bethany Letiecq, and Gabriel Winant, "The University of the Future: An Interview with United Faculty for the Common Good," *N+1*, April 18, 2024, https://www.nplusonemag.com/online-only/online-only/the-university-of-the-future/; Douglas Belkin, "Why Americans Have Lost Faith in the Value of College Three Generations of 'College for All' in the U.S. Has Left Most Families Looking for Alternatives," *Wall Street Journal*, January 19, 2024, https://www.wsj.com/us-news/education/why-americans-have-lost-faith-in-the-value-of-college-b6b635f2; Donald Earl Collins, "The Great Collapse of US Higher Education Has Begun," *Al Jazeera*, April 24, 2025, https://www.aljazeera.com/opinions/2025/4/24/the-great-collapse-of-us-higher-education-has-begun.

Introduction

1. "Open Doors 2024 Annual Data Release," 2024, https://opendoorsdata.org/open-doors-2024-annual-data-release/.
2. "Educational Institutions," Fast Facts, National Center for Education Statistics (NCES), n.d., https://nces.ed.gov/fastfacts/display.asp?id=1122.
3. Adam Tooze, "Chartbook 313: Being Realistic in the Polycrisis? Or, Does the West/Global North Know What Time It Is?," *Chartbook*, Substack, August 31, 2024, https://adamtooze.substack.com/p/chartbook-313-being-realistic-in.
4. David F. Labaree, *A Perfect Mess: The Unlikely Ascendancy of American Higher Education* (University of Chicago Press, 2017).
5. John Ross, "Australian Universities Consider Mergers," *Inside Higher Ed*, July 14, 2023, https://www.insidehighered.com/news/global/2023/07/14/australian-universities-consider-mergers; John Gerritsen, "New Zealand Universities Face Severe Financial Challenges," *University World News*, February 2, 2024, https://www.universityworldnews.com/post.php?story=20240202121727875; Gero Federkeil, "The Expansion of German HE Has Come to an End. Now What?," *University World News*, March 30, 2024, https://www.universityworldnews.com/post.php?story=20240326080707213. Tom Williams, "Falling Demand Quashes Hopes for British Enrollment Growth," *Inside Higher Ed*, October 25, 2024, https://www.insidehighered.com/news/admissions/traditional-age/2024/10/25/falling-demand-quashes-hopes-enrollment-growth-britain.
6. For an influential description of the polycrisis model, see Adam Tooze, "Chartbook #130 Defining Polycrisis—from Crisis Pictures to the Crisis Matrix," *Chartbook*,

Substack, June 24, 2022, https://adamtooze.substack.com/p/chartbook-130-defining-polycrisis.

7. Bryan Alexander, "'The Professors Are the Enemy': J. D. Vance on Higher Education," blog, July 18, 2024, https://bryanalexander.org/politics/the-professors-are-the-enemy-j-d-vance-on-higher-education; Paul Dans and Steven Groves, eds., *Mandate for Leadership: The Conservative Promise* (The Heritage Foundation, 2023).
8. For peak library book circulation, one recent reflection is Steven Mintz, "The Evolving University Library: What's Gained, What's Lost," *Inside Higher Ed*, October 28, 2024, https://www.insidehighered.com/opinion/blogs/higher-ed-gamma/2024/10/28/whats-gained-whats-lost-evolving-university-library; David Fickling, "Peak Beef Could Already Be Here," *Bloomberg*, October 29, 2024, https://www.bloomberg.com/opinion/articles/2024-10-29/carbon-hoofprint-peak-beef-could-already-be-here. Peak oil remains elusive and controversial. One update: Jean Laherrère, Charles A.S. Hall, and Roger Bentley, "How Much Oil Remains for the World to Produce? Comparing Assessment Methods, and Separating Fact from Fiction," *Current Research in Environmental Sustainability* 4 (2022), 100174, https://doi.org/10.1016/j.crsust.2022.100174. Another thinks that oil production might not have passed peak, but oil trade and shipping have, as the polycrisis might force more nations to a mix of local supply with renewables: Jeff Currie, "The New Joule Order," Carlyle, March 10, 2025, https://www.carlyle.com/global-insights/research/the-new-joule-order.
9. Bryan Alexander, "Peak Education 2013," blog, September 18, 2013, https://bryanalexander.org/uncategorized/peak-education-2013/; Bryan Alexander, "Has Higher Ed Peaked?" *Inside Higher Ed*, April 06, 2014, https://www.insidehighered.com/views/2014/04/07/essay-considers-whether-higher-education-us-has-peaked.

1. *Peak Higher Education, the First Decade*

1. "Educational Institutions," Fast Facts, National Center for Education Statistics (NCES), n.d., https://nces.ed.gov/fastfacts/display.asp?id=1122; "Table 303.10. Total Fall Enrollment in Degree-Granting Postsecondary Institutions, by Attendance Status, Sex of Student, and Control of Institution: Selected Years, 1947 through 2031," Digest of Educational Statistics, National Center for Education Statistics (NCES), n.d., https://nces.ed.gov/programs/digest/d22/tables/dt22_303.10.asp.
2. Brian C. Mitchell and W. Joseph King, *How to Run a College: A Practical Guide for Trustees, Faculty, Administrators, and Policymakers* (Johns Hopkins University Press, 2018), 37.
3. "Annual NACUBO Tuition Discounting Study Finds Financial Aid Awards and Undergraduate Enrollment on the Rise at Private Colleges and Universities," news release, National Association of College and University Business Officers (NACUBO), May 14, 2024, https://www.nacubo.org/Press-Releases/2024/Annual-NACUBO-Tuition-Discounting-Study-Finds-Financial-Aid-Awards-on-the-Rise.
4. Bryan Alexander, "When Will the First College or University Charge Six Figures Per Year? A 2024 Update," blog, May 13, 2024, https://bryanalexander.org/economics/when-will-the-first-college-or-university-charge-six-figures-per-year-a-2024

-update/. The ranking as of that date: University of Southern California, $95,225; Northwestern University, $94,878 ($86,397 for resident assistants; $76,674 if living with relatives and commuting); Colorado College, $94,866 ($91,154 if students waive campus health plan); Vanderbilt University, $94,051 (my calculation; page didn't publish total); New York University, $93,184 ($74,932 for commuters); Harvey Mudd College, $93,131; Wesleyan University, $92,994 ("[frosh]/$92,694 [continuing students]"); Stanford University, $92,892; Vassar College, $92,580; Washington University in St. Louis, $92,523; University of Pennsylvania, $92,288 ($91,474 for living off campus; $76,076, living with family); Cornell University, $92,150; Wellesley College, $92,060; Amherst College, $91,930 (not including personal expenses or transportation; assuming the health care and tuition insurances aren't waived); Brown University, $91,676; Claremont McKenna College, $91,510; Dartmouth College, $91,312; Wake Forest University, $91,266; Kenyon College, $91,010; Yale University, $90,975; CalTech, $90,822 (off-campus is higher at $94,380; living with parents is lower at $82,878); Barnard College, $90,928; Boston University, $90,207; and Franklin & Marshall College, $90,079.

5. John Marcus, "The Number of 18-Year-Olds Is about to Drop Sharply, Packing a Wallop for Colleges—and the Economy," *Hechinger Report*, January 8, 2025, https://hechingerreport.org/the-impact-of-this-is-economic-decline.
6. "Table 303.70. Total Undergraduate Fall Enrollment in Degree-Granting Postsecondary Institutions, by Attendance Status, Sex of Student, and Control and Level of Institution: Selected Years, 1970 through 2031," Digest of Education Statistics, National Center for Education Statistics (NCES), n.d., https://nces.ed.gov/programs/digest/d23/tables/dt23_303.70.asp.
7. For term enrollment estimates from 2012 to 2023, see https://nscresearchcenter.org/. The center seems to have revised its methodology recently. We can track one string of numbers from their publications as follows:

2010	20,510,526
2011	20,556,272
2012	20,195,924
2013	19,885,203
2014	19,619,773
2015	19,280,473
2016	19,010,459
2017	18,811,280
2018	18,482,391
2019	18,239,874
2020	17,778,484
2021	17,302,364

8. "Educational Institutions"; "A look at Trends in College Consolidation Since 2016," *Higher Ed Dive*, updated Dec. 5, 2024, https://www.highereddive.com/news/how-many-colleges-and-universities-have-closed-since-2016/539379/. See also this visualization, after NCES data: "Number of Closures of Degree-Granting

Postsecondary Institutions in the United States, 1969–2021," HolonIQ, May 30, 2023, https://index.holoniq.com/charts/HCH4RZNM3YRYPIRNUFPT/Number-of-closures-of-degree-granting-postsecondary-institutions-in-the-United-States%252C-1969-2021; "The Total Number of Higher Education Institutions Decreases by 2 Percent," National Center for Education Statistics (NCES), August 21, 2024, https://nces.ed.gov/whatsnew/press_releases/8_21_2024.asp#:~:text=During%20the%202023%E2%80%9324%20academic,granting%20institutions%20in%202023%E2%80%9324%2C.

9. Laura Brown, Maya Dayan, Brenna McLaughlin, Roger C. Schonfeld, John Sherer, and Erich van Rijn, "Print Revenue and Open Access Monographs A University Press Study," Ithaka S+R, September 19, 2023, https://doi.org/10.18665/sr.319642.

10. Benjamin M. Schmidt, "The History BA since the Great Recession: The 2018 AHA Majors Report," American Historical Association, November 26, 2018, https://www.historians.org/perspectives-article/the-history-ba-since-the-great-recession-the-2018-aha-majors-report-december-2018/; Nathan Heller, "The End of the English Major Enrollment in the Humanities Is in Free Fall at Colleges Around the Country. What Happened?" *New Yorker*, February 27, 2023, https://www.newyorker.com/magazine/2023/03/06/the-end-of-the-english-major; Rachael Scarborough King and Seth Rudy, *The Ends of Knowledge: Outcomes and Endpoints Across the Arts and Sciences* (Bloomsbury Academic, 2023). "Number of Staff at Title IV Institutions and Administrative Offices, by Control and Level of Institution, Medical School Staff Status, Occupational Catery [*sic*], and Employment Status: United States, Fall 2012," Integrated Postsecondary Education Data System (IPEDS), n.d., https://nces.ed.gov/ipeds/search?surveyComponents=Fall%20Enrollment%20(EF)&overlayTableId=11366. From that site, I derived this list of workers over a decade: 2023–4 4,029,311

2022–3	3,935,708
2021–2	3,873,739
2020–1	3,868,066
2019–20	4,023,596
2018–19	3,986,129
2017–18	3,979,018
2016–17	3,970,842
2015–16	3,981,632
2014–15	4,128,462
2013–14	3,969,226
2012–13	3,945,124.

Then the 2022 release revised previous numbers, while adding new ones:

2017	19949828
2018	19393441
2019	19265402
2020	18757555
2021	18287747

2022 18155612
2023 18331612
2024 19148612.

I have not been able to receive clarification on this from the Center, but the revised numbers nonetheless show the same trendline as previous ones did.

11. Richard Arum and Josipa Roksa, *Academically Adrift: Limited Learning on College Campuses* (University of Chicago Press, 2011). See also "Measuring the Student Experience," posted April 1, 2021, by Bryan Alexander, YouTube, 57 min., 15 sec., https://youtu.be/cxx8tVfD4Hg?si=P3IW1Dc_jE3qJULj.
12. Anna Brown, "Most Americans Say Higher Ed Is Heading in Wrong Direction, but Partisans Disagree on Why," Pew Research, July 26, 2018, https://www.pewresearch.org/short-reads/2018/07/26/most-americans-say-higher-ed-is-heading-in-wrong-direction-but-partisans-disagree-on-why/; Stephanie Marken, "Half in U.S. Now Consider College Education Very Important," Gallup, December 12, 2019, archived at https://web.archive.org/web/20200103123753/https://news.gallup.com/poll/270008/half-consider-college-education-important.aspx.
13. Stephanie Marken, "About a Quarter of U.S. Adults Consider Higher Ed Affordable," Gallup, January 7, 2020, https://www.gallup.com/education/272366/quarter-adults-consider-higher-affordable.aspx; Jeffrey M. Jones, "U.S. Confidence in Higher Education Now Closely Divided," Gallup, July 8, 2024, https://news.gallup.com/poll/646880/confidence-higher-education-closely-divided.aspx.
14. "2024 Parent Survey: Understanding Top Parent Concerns in College Search," Enroll360, EAB, 2024, https://attachment.eab.com/wp-content/uploads/2024/08/PDF-ES-Enroll360-Parent-Survey-Insight-Paper.pdf. I credit the "academia as debt generator" phrase to Glen McGee.
15. "Student Debt," Federal Reserve Bank of New York, n.d., https://www.newyorkfed.org/microeconomics/topics/student-debt; Melanie Hanson, "Student Loan Debt Statistics," Education Data Initiative, March 16, 2025, https://educationdata.org/student-loan-debt-statistics; Adam Looney and Constantine Yannelis, "What Went Wrong with Federal Student Loans?" *Journal of Economic Perspectives* 38, no. 3 (2024): 209–36, https://www.aeaweb.org/articles?id=10.1257/jep.38.3.209; "Ensuring a Living Wage Through Higher Education," The HEA Group, February 20, 2024, https://www.theheagroup.com/blog/ensuring-a-living-wage-through-higher-education.
16. Ben Unglesbee, "'We Can't Cut Anymore': Can Colleges Recover from the Gut-Punch of Inflation?" *Higher Ed Dive*, July 1, 2024, https://www.highereddive.com/news/can-colleges-recover-from-the-gut-punch-of-inflation/720214/.
17. Neil Kraus, *The Fantasy Economy: Neoliberalism, Inequality, and the Education Reform Movement* (Temple University Press, 2024); "Higher Education and the Fantasy Economy," posted February 23, 2024, by Bryan Alexander, YouTube, 55 min. 44 sec., https://youtu.be/-XFexUU6BLg?si=yOjtczEVDVkoqew-; "Do Adults Have the Skills They Need to Thrive in a Changing World? Survey of Adult Skills 2023," The Organisation of Economic Cooperation and Development (OECD), Skills Studies, December 10, 2024, https://doi.org/10.1787/b263dc5d-en; Gary Roth,

The Educated Underclass: Students and the Promise of Social Mobility (Pluto Press, 2019). I believe this is the first appearance of the college meltdown term: Dahn Shaulis, "Forecasting the US College Meltdown," *Higher Education Inquirer*, December 15, 2016, https://www.highereducationinquirer.org/2016/12/predictive-models-of-us-college-meltdown.html.

18. Danielle Douglas-Gabriel, interview with author, January 22, 2025.
19. Melissa Korn and Matt Barnum, "Bloomberg's $140 Million Push to Get Lower-Income Students Into Top Colleges Falls Short," *Wall Street Journal*, September 23, 2024, https://www.wsj.com/us-news/education/bloombergs-140-million-push-to-get-lower-income-students-into-top-colleges-falls-short-3839b520.

2. Forces Pushing Academia Further Downslope

Epigraph: "J. D. Vance: 'The Universities are the Enemy," National Conservatism Conference II," posted November 2, 2021, by National Conservatism, YouTube, 30 min., 54 sec., https://youtu.be/oFR65Cifnhw?si=ZBpmdHXrqNz7tbCn. To be fair, at the time of the speech he was neither vice president nor a candidate for that position.

1. I owe a debt to this paper for its excellent data gathering and analysis: Robert J. Kelchen, Dubravka Ritter, and Douglas A. Webber, "Predicting College Closures and Financial Distress," Working Paper No. 33216 (National Bureau of Economic Research [NBER]), November, 2024), https://doi.org.10.3386/w33216.
2. Jon Marcus, "In Japan, Plummeting University Enrollment Forecasts What's Ahead for the U.S." *Hechinger Report*, April 18, 2023, https://hechingerreport.org/in-japan-plummeting-university-enrollment-forecasts-whats-ahead-for-the-u-s/; Sayaka Saito, "59% of Japan's Private Universities Miss Quotas for New Enrollment," *Nikkei Asia*, September 14, 2024, https://asia.nikkei.com/Business/Education/59-of-Japan-s-private-universities-miss-quotas-for-new-enrollment; GBD 2021 Fertility and Forecasting Collaborators, "Global Fertility in 204 Countries and Territories, 1950–2021, with Forecasts to 2100: A Comprehensive Demographic Analysis for the Global Burden of Disease Study 2021," *The Lancet* 403, no. 10440 (2024): 2057–99, https://www.thelancet.com/journals/lancet/article/PIIS0140-6736(24)00550-6/fulltext.
3. Brady E. Hamilton, Joyce A. Martin, and Michelle J.K. Osterman, *Births: Provisional Data for 2023*, NVSS Vital Statistics Rapid Release, no. 35 (April 2024). National Center for Health Statistics. https://www.cdc.gov/nchs/data/vsrr/vsrr035.pdf; Kristie Wilder, "New 2024 Population Estimates Show Nation's Population Grew by About 1% to 340.1 Million Since 2023," United States Census Bureau, December 19, 2024, https://www.census.gov/library/stories/2024/12/population-estimates.html.
4. Hagai Levine, Niels Jørgensen, Anderson Martino-Andrade et al., "Temporal Trends in Sperm Count: A Systematic Review and Meta-Regression Analysis," *Human Reproduction Update* 23, no. 6 (2017): 646–59, https://doi.org/10.1093/humupd/dmx022; Hagai Levine, Niels Jørgensen, Anderson Martino-Andrade

et al., "Temporal Trends in Sperm Count: A Systematic Review and Meta-Regression Analysis of Samples Collected Globally in the 20th and 21st Centuries," *Human Reproduction Update* 29, no. 2 (March 1, 2023): 157–76, https://doi.org/10.1093/humupd/dmac035; Marwa Lahimer, Maria Abou Diwan, Debbie Montjean et al., "Endocrine Disrupting Chemicals and Male Fertility: From Physiological to Molecular Effects," *Frontiers in Public Health* 11 (October 9, 2023), https://doi.org/10.3389/fpubh.2023.1232646; Blake Vessa, Barry Perlman, Peter G. McGovern, and Sara S. Morelli, "Endocrine Disruptors and Female Fertility: A Review of Pesticide and Plasticizer Effects," *Fertility and Sterility Reports* 3, no. 2 (2022): 86–90, https://doi.org/10.1016/j.xfre.2022.04.003.

5. Nathan D. Grawe, *Demographics and the Demand for Higher Education* (Johns Hopkins University Press, 2018). See also our Future Trends Forum discussion with Grawe: "Demographics and Education's Future, with Nathan Grawe," posted March 20, 2018, by Bryan Alexander, YouTube, March 20, 2018, 60 min., 10 secs., https://youtu.be/oUFosgQ3Hok?si=DAanvEnlhiacheos.
6. Patrick Lane, Colleen Falkenstern, and Peace Bransberger, *Knocking at the College Door: Projections of High School Graduates* (Western Interstate Commission for Higher Education, December 2024), https://www.wiche.edu/wp-content/uploads/2024/12/2024-Knocking-at-the-College-Door-final.pdf.
7. Bryan Alexander, "When Will the First College or University Charge Six Figures Per Year? A 2024 Update," blog, May 13, 2024, https://bryanalexander.org/economics/when-will-the-first-college-or-university-charge-six-figures-per-year-a-2024-update/.
8. Ben Unglesbee, "'We Can't Cut Anymore': Can Colleges Recover from the Gut-Punch of Inflation?" *Higher Ed Dive*, July 1, 2024, https://www.highereddive.com/news/can-colleges-recover-from-the-gut-punch-of-inflation/720214/.
9. Kasia Lundy, Haven Ladd, and Miriam El-Baz, "IVM Finds Heightened Risk in Higher Education as Stimulus Funds Expire," EY Parthenon, February 23, 2024, https://www.ey.com/en_us/insights/education/strategy-consulting-higher-ed-financial-risk-as-funds-expire.
10. Jessica L Wood and Adam J Gillespie, "Outlook For Global Not-For-Profit Higher Education: Credit Quality Divergence Continues," S&P Global, December 7, 2023, https://www.spglobal.com/ratings/en/research/articles/231207-outlook-for-global-not-for-profit-higher-education-credit-quality-divergence-continues-12927541; "Heightened Cash Monitoring," Federal Student Aid, n.d., https://studentaid.gov/data-center/school/hcm.
11. Brian Kennedy and Alec Tyson, "Americans' Trust in Scientists, Positive Views of Science Continue to Decline," Pew Research Center, November 14, 2023, https://www.pewresearch.org/science/2023/11/14/americans-trust-in-scientists-positive-views-of-science-continue-to-decline/.
12. Richard Fry, Dana Braga, and Kim Parker, "Is College Worth It? As Economic Outcomes for Young Adults With and Without Degrees Have Improved, Americans Hold Mixed Views on the Value Of College," Pew Research Center, May 23, 2024, https://www.pewresearch.org/social-trends/2024/05/23/is-college-worth-it-2/.

13. Nathan Honeycutt, "Confidence in Colleges and Universities Hits New Lows, per FIRE Polls," FIRE, June 11, 2024, https://www.thefire.org/news/confidence-colleges-and-universities-hits-new-lows-fire-polls.
14. "J. D. Vance: 'The Universities are the Enemy," National Conservatism Conference II," posted November 2, 2021, by National Conservatism, YouTube, 30 min., 54 sec., https://youtu.be/oFR65Cifnhw?si=ZBpmdHXrqNz7tbCn.
15. "J.D. Vance | The Universities are the Enemy," Project 2025 | Presidential Transition Project, n.d., https://www.project2025.org/.
16. Josh Moody, "Moody's Downgrades Sector Outlook to Negative," *Inside Higher Ed*, March 19, 2025, https://www.insidehighered.com/news/business/financial-health/2025/03/19/moodys-downgrades-sector-outlook-negative.
17. Eric Kelderman, "The Lure of Work," *Chronicle of Higher Education*, June 3, 2024, https://www.chronicle.com/article/the-lure-of-work.
18. Ashley Mowreader, "Survey: Over Half of Rising Seniors Feel Pessimistic About Starting Their Careers," *Inside Higher Ed*, August 22, 2024, https://www.insidehighered.com/news/student-success/life-after-college/2024/08/22/class-2025-say-market-student-loan-debt-impact.
19. Leila Bengali, Marcus Sander, Robert G. Valletta, and Cindy Zhao, "Falling College Wage Premiums by Race and Ethnicity," Federal Reserve Bank of San Francisco, August 28, 2023, https://www.frbsf.org/economic-research/publications/economic-letter/2023/august/falling-college-wage-premiums-by-race-and-ethnicity; William R. Emmons, Ana Hernández Kent, and Lowell R. Ricketts, "Is College Still Worth It? The New Calculus of Falling Returns," Federal Reserve Bank of St. Louis *Review* 101, no. 4 (2019): 297–329. https://doi.org/10.20955/r.101.297-329, October 15, 2019; David Autor, Arindrajit Dube, and Annie McGrew, "The Unexpected Compression: Competition At Work In The Low Wage Labor Market," Working Paper No. 31010 (National Bureau of Economic Research [NBER]), http://www.nber.org/papers/w31010; Michael Itzkowitz, *Some Graduate Schools Never Pay Off* (Student Defense and The HEA Group, July 2023), https://static1.squarespace.com/static/63617bfab00c640904baab4c/t/64c7f9b8a878c86495ab4ad9/1690827193148/NSLDN_BRIEF_Some+Grad+Schools_B.pdf.
20. "Table 303.70. Total Undergraduate Fall Enrollment in Degree-Granting Postsecondary Institutions, by Attendance Status, Sex of Student, and Control and Level of Institution: Selected Years, 1970 Through 2031,"Digest of Educational Statistics, National Center for Education Statistics (NCES), n.d., https://nces.ed.gov/programs/digest/d22/tables/dt22_303.70.asp; Richard Reeves and Will Secker, "Degrees of Difference: Male College Enrollment and Completion," American Institute for Boys and Men (AIBM), March 29, 2024, https://aibm.org/research/male-college-enrollment-and-completion/; Richard Fry, "Fewer Young Men Are in College, Especially at 4-Year Schools," Pew Research Center, December 18, 2023, https://www.pewresearch.org/short-reads/2023/12/18/fewer-young-men-are-in-college-especially-at-4-year-schools/; Celeste Davis, "Why Aren't We Talking About the Real Reason Male College Enrollment Is Dropping? We Would Rather Talk About Literally Everything Else," *Matriarchal Blessing*,

Substack, October 6, 2024, https://celestemdavis.substack.com/p/why-boys-dont-go-to-college.

21. Nicholas Bloom, Charles I. Jones, John Van Reenen, and Michael Webb, "Are Ideas Getting Harder To Find?," Working Paper No. 23782 (National Bureau of Economic Research [NBER]), November 2024), http://www.nber.org/papers/w23782. This does a good job of summarizing research and correcting a meme: Sierra Williams, "Are 90% of Academic Papers Really Never Cited? Reviewing the Literature on Academic Citations," *LSE Impact Blog*, London School of Economics, April 23, 2014, https://blogs.lse.ac.uk/impactofsocialsciences/2014/04/23/academic-papers-citation-rates-remler/; Richard Van Noorden, "The Science That's Never Been Cited," *Nature*, last updated February 2, 2018, https://www.nature.com/articles/d41586-017-08404-0.
22. Kevin Kelly, Kathryn E. Linder, and Thomas J. Tobin, *Going Alt-Ac: A Guide to Alternative Academic Careers* (Routledge, 2020).
23. Peter Turchin, *End Times: Elites, Counter-Elites, and the Path of Political Disintegration* (Penguin, 2023); Noah Smith, "America Is Pumping Out Too Many Ph.D.s," Bloomberg, January 4, 2021, https://web.archive.org/web/20210113115056/https://www.bloomberg.com/opinion/articles/2021-01-04/america-is-pumping-out-too-many-ph-d-s.

3. *After the Consensus Shattered*

Epigraph: Karissa Waddick, "'Adult Money' and No College Debt: Harris and Trump Back Alternative Routes to Good Jobs," *USA Today*, last updated October 14, 2024, https://www.usatoday.com/story/news/politics/elections/2024/09/29/harris-trump-college-jobs/74967902007/.

1. Kalen Goodluck, Tristan Ahtone and Robert Lee, "The Land-Grant Universities Still Profiting Off Indigenous Homelands," *High Country News*, August 18, 2020, https://www.hcn.org/articles/indigenous-affairs-the-land-grant-universities-still-profiting-off-indigenous-homelands/.
2. "Table 301.20. Historical Summary of Faculty, Enrollment, Degrees Conferred, and Finances in Degree-Granting Postsecondary Institutions: Selected Academic Years, 1869–70 Through 2020–21," Digest of Educational Statistics, National Center for Education Statistics (NCES), n.d., https://nces.ed.gov/programs/digest/d22/tables/dt22_301.20.asp.
3. Jerome Tuccille, *The War Against the Vets: The World War I Bonus Army During the Great Depression* (Potomac Books, 2018).
4. "Remarks at Southwest Texas State College Upon Signing the Higher Education Act of 1965," LBJ for Kids!, LBJ Presidential Library, n.d., https://web.archive.org/web/20070714005531/http://www.lbjlib.utexas.edu/johnson/lbjforkids/edu_whca370-text.shtm.
5. "Background: President Clinton's Proposal To Make College Education More Affordable For Families," National Archives, n.d., https://clintonwhitehouse3.archives.gov/WH/old.SOTU00/education_bg.html; "Table 303.70, Total

Undergraduate Fall Enrollment in Degree-Granting Postsecondary Institutions, by Attendance Status, Sex Of Student, and Control and Level of Institution: Selected Years, 1970 Through 2031," Digest of Educational Statistics, National Center for Education Statistics (NCES), n.d., https://nces.ed.gov/programs/digest/d23/tables/dt23_303.70.asp; "Table 301.20"; Philip G. Altbach, "Patterns of Higher Education Development," in *American Higher Education in the Twenty-First Century: Social, Political, and Economic Changes*, 4th ed., ed. Michael N. Bastedo, Philip G. Altbach, and Patricia J. Gumport (Johns Hopkins University Press, 2016), 197.

6. Hieu Nguyen, "Free College? Assessing Enrollment Responses to the Tennessee Promise Program," *Labour Economics* 66 (October 2020), https://doi.org/10.1016/j.labeco.2020.101882; "Jayapal and Sanders Introduce College for All Act," Pramila Jayapal, Congresswoman for WA-07, April 21, 2021, https://jayapal.house.gov/2021/04/21/college-for-all/; Helen Santoro, "Tax Ivy League Endowments, and Fund Public Higher Ed," *Jacobin*, February 26, 2024, https://jacobin.com/2024/02/tax-ivy-league-endowments-public-university-massachusetts/; Amelia Benavides-Colón, "Free Community College Just Keeps Growing. Here's the Latest," *Chronicle of Higher Education*, August 23, 2024, https://www.chronicle.com/article/free-community-college-just-keeps-growing-heres-the-latest.
7. "Remarks of President Barack Obama—Address to Joint Session of Congress," The White House, President Barack Obama, February 24, 2009, https://obama whitehouse.archives.gov/the-press-office/remarks-president-barack-obama-address-joint-session-congress.
8. "Table 303.70" and "Table 301.20"; "CPS Historical Time Series Tables," The United States Census, last revised February 12, 2025, https://www.census.gov/data/tables/time-series/demo/educational-attainment/cps-historical-time-series.html.
9. David A. Bergeron and Carmel Martin, "Strengthening Our Economy Through College for All," The Center for American Progress (CAP), February 19, 2015, https://www.americanprogress.org/article/strengthening-our-economy-through-college-for-all/; Donald Harward, "Engaged Learning and the Core Purposes of Liberal Education," *Liberal Education* 93, no. 1 (2007), https://bttop.org/wp-content/uploads/2020/09/Harward-Engaged-Learning-and-the-Core-Purposes-. . . on-of-American-Colleges-Universities.pdf;
10. Tressie McMillan Cottom, *Lower Ed: The Troubling Rise of For-Profit Colleges in the New Economy* (The New Press, 2018), 12.
11. Scott Carlson, "Should Everyone Go to College? For Poor Kids, 'College for All' Isn't The Mantra It Was Meant to Be," *Chronicle of Higher Education*, May 1, 2016, https://www.chronicle.com/article/should-everyone-go-to-college/.
12. Douglas Belkin, "Americans Are Losing Faith in College Education, WSJ-NORC Poll Finds," *Wall Street Journal*, March 31, 2023, https://www.wsj.com/articles/americans-are-losing-faith-in-college-education-wsj-norc-poll-finds-3a836ce1.
13. Virginia Foxx, "The Dangers of the College Degree-for-All Mentality," *National Review*, July 3, 2023, https://www.nationalreview.com/2023/07/the-dangers-of-the-college-degree-for-all-mentality/.

14. Stateline, "Three Months After Reform Announcement, Maryland Will Hire You—No College Degree Required," *Maryland Matters*, June 27, 2022, https://marylandmatters.org/2022/06/27/three-months-after-reform-announcement-maryland-will-hire-you-no-college-degree-required/; "Governor Shapiro Leads the Nation on Eliminating College Degree Requirements, Expanding Job Opportunities," Commonwealth of Pennsylvania, March 01, 2023, https://www.pa.gov/governor/newsroom/press-releases/governor-shapiro-leads-the-nation-on-eliminating-college-degree-.html; Nathan M. Greenfield, "This State Is Hiring: Bachelor Degree Holders Need Not Apply," *University World News*, May 6, 2024, https://www.universityworldnews.com/post.php?story=20240503201654237. I summarize other cases here: Bryan Alexander, "Massachusetts Removes College Degree Requirements from Most State Jobs," blog, February 14, 2024, https://bryanalexander.org/future-of-education/massachusetts-removes-college-degree-requirements-from-most-state-jobs/.
15. Sean Collins Walsh, "Mayor Cherelle Parker Wants to Diversify the City's Workforce, and She Thinks Some Civil Service Rules Get in the Way," *Philadelphia Inquirer*, February 27, 2024, https://www.inquirer.com/politics/philadelphia/philadelphia-hiring-practices-cherelle-parker-20240227.html.
16. Rachel Cohen, "Stop Requiring College Degrees for Jobs That Don't Need Them," *Vox*, March 19, 2023, https://www.vox.com/policy/23628627/degree-inflation-college-bacheors-stars-labor-worker-paper-ceiling.
17. Joe Lischwe, Alex Noether, Maria Gordian, Andrea D'Arcy, and Jon Barfield, "Eliminate a Degree of Difficulty: Hire for Skills, Not School," Bain & Company, February 2023, https://www.bain.com/insights/eliminate-a-degree-of-difficulty-hire-for-skills-not-school/; Kate Tornone, "Walmart Scraps Degree Requirements for Some Corporate Jobs," *Higher Ed Dive*, October 5, 2023, https://www.highereddive.com/news/walmart-removes-degree-requirement-headquarters-jobs/695540/; "Nearly Half of Companies Plan to Eliminate Bachelor's Degree Requirements in 2024," Intelligent, July 23, 2024, https://www.intelligent.com/nearly-half-of-companies-plan-to-eliminate-bachelors-degree-requirements-in-2024/.
18. "Fact Sheet: Biden-Harris Administration Announces Record Federal Investments in Registered Apprenticeships, Holds Workforce Hub Convening in Philadelphia with New Commitments to Train and Hire Residents to Work on Major Infrastructure Projects," statement, The White House, July 11, 2024, https://bidenwhitehouse.archives.gov/briefing-room/statements-releases/2024/07/11/fact-sheet-biden-%E2%81%A0harris-administration-announces-record-federal-investments-in-registered-apprenticeships-holds-workforce-hub-convening-in-philadelphia-with-new-commitments-to-train-and-hir/.
19. "Fact Sheet."
20. Jeff Mason and Kanishka Singh, "Kamala Harris Says She Will Cut Degree Requirements for Certain Federal Jobs," Reuters, September 14, 2024, https://www.reuters.com/world/us/kamala-harris-says-she-will-cut-degree-requirements-certain-federal-jobs-2024-09-14/; *A New Way Forward for The Middle Class*, n.d., https://web.archive.org/web/20241101015248/https://kamalaharris.com/wp-content

/uploads/2024/09/Policy_Book_Economic-Opportunity.pdf; Barack Obama (@BarackObama), "Here's an example of a smart policy that gets rid of unnecessary college degree requirements and reduces barriers to good paying jobs. I hope other states follow suit!," X, March 19, 2023, https://x.com/BarackObama/status/1637574955637383171.

21. "Virginia Joins the Movement against Credentialism," *National Review*, June 2, 2023, https://www.nationalreview.com/2023/06/virginia-joins-the-movement-against-credentialism/.
22. Project 2025 Tracker, n.d., https://www.project2025.observer/.
23. Eric Kelderman, "College for All? Not Anymore," *Chronicle of Higher Education*, September 4, 2024, https://www.chronicle.com/article/college-for-all-not-anymore.
24. Te-Ping Chen, "The Schools Reviving Shop Class Offer a Hedge Against the AI Future," *Wall Street Journal*, March 1, 2025, https://www.wsj.com/us-news/education/high-school-shop-class-revival-24d7a525.

4. *Automation Comes for the Campus*

Epigraph: Palmer Luckey (@PalmerLuckey), "What will happen in broader academia when clear scientific consensus is that AI-assisted education delivers better outcomes than 3.8M teachers currently do?," X, February 15, 2025, https://x.com/PalmerLuckey/status/1890904808233603242; Elon Musk (@elonmusk), "That is already possible," February 15, 2025, https://x.com/elonmusk/status/1890905182516461608.

1. Kevin Kelly, *What Technology Wants* (Viking, 2010).
2. *2001: A Space Odyssey* (1968) and *Colossus: The Forbin Project* (1970) offer much more interesting and useful film examples than *Terminator*, but apparently lack the cultural cachet. There is even a computer game you can play to simulate that paperclip apocalypse: https://www.decisionproblem.com/paperclips/.
3. Carlota Perez, *Technological Revolutions and Financial Capital: The Dynamics of Bubbles and Golden Ages* (Edward Elgar Publishing, 2002).
4. For one unusually open example of a dataset containing copious amounts of intellectual property, see Kevin Schaul, Szu Yu Chen, and Nitasha Tiku, "Inside the Secret List of Websites That Make AI Like ChatGPT Sound Smart," *Washington Post*, April 19, 2023, https://www.washingtonpost.com/technology/interactive/2023/ai-chatbot-learning/.
5. Shiona McCallum, "ChatGPT Banned in Italy over Privacy Concerns," BBC, April 1, 2023, https://www.bbc.com/news/technology-65139406; Elvira Pollina and Alvise Armellini, "Italy Fines OpenAI over ChatGPT Privacy Rules Breach," Reuters, December 20, 2024. https://www.reuters.com/technology/italy-fines-openai-15-million-euros-over-privacy-rules-breach-2024-12-20/.
6. Maha Bali, "Different Critiques of AI in Education," *Reflecting Allowed* (blog), December 22, 2024, https://blog.mahabali.me/educational-technology-2/different-critiques-of-ai-in-education/; Julie Ray, "Americans Express Real Concerns About

Artificial Intelligence: Few Trust Businesses to Use It Responsibly, but Transparency Could Help," Gallup, August 27, 2024, https://news.gallup.com/poll/648953/americans-express-real-concerns-artificial-intelligence.aspx.

7. Jim Dator, "Alternative Futures at the Manoa School," *Journal of Futures Studies* 14, no. 2 (2009): 1–18; Jim Dator, "Manoa's Four Generic Images of the Futures," *APF Compass*, July 2017, 2–6, https://contrabass-accordion-eyx2.squarespace.com/s/4-Dator-4-Futures-Museum.pdf.
8. Emily M. Bender, Timnit Gebru, Angelina McMillan-Major, and Shmargaret Shmitchell, "On the Dangers of Stochastic Parrots: Can Language Models Be Too Big?," in *FAccT '21: Proceedings of the 2021 ACM Conference on Fairness, Accountability, and Transparency* (Association for Computing Machinery), 610–23, https://dl.acm.org/doi/10.1145/3442188.3445922; Jennifer Sano-Franchini, Megan McIntyre, and Maggie Fernandes, "Refusing GenAI in Writing Studies: A Quickstart Guide," n.d., https://refusinggenai.wordpress.com/; Siva Vaidhyanathan, "My students are using AI to cheat. Here's why it's a teachable moment," The Guardian, May 19, 2023, https://www.theguardian.com/technology/2023/may/18/ai-cheating-teaching-chatgpt-students-college-university.
9. Neal Stephenson, *The Diamond Age: Or, A Young Lady's Illustrated Primer* (Bantam Spectra, 1995), for a very influential example of an automated tutor.

5. *The Anthropocene Is Here, Ready or Not*

1. Timothy Morton, *Hyperobjects: Philosophy and Ecology After the End of the World* (University of Minnesota Press, 2013); Bryan Alexander, *Universities on Fire: Higher Education in the Climate Crisis* (Johns Hopkins University Press, 2023).
2. "Greenland's Glaciers Melting Twice as Fast as They Were 20 Years Ago," *Yale Environment 360*, November 10, 2023, https://e360.yale.edu/digest/greenland-glaciers-melting-climate-change; Wim Thiery, Stefan Lange, Joeri Rogelj et al., "Intergenerational Inequities in Exposure to Climate Extremes: Young Generations Are Severely Threatened by Climate Change," *Science* 374, no. 6564 (2021): 158–160, https://doi.org/10.1126/science.abi733; Corbin Hiar, "Big Banks Predict Catastrophic Warming, with Profit Potential," *E&E News*, March 31, 2025, https://www.eenews.net/articles/big-banks-predict-catastrophic-warming-with-profit-potential/; "WMO Confirms 2024 as Warmest Year on Record at About 1.55°C Above Pre-Industrial Level," The World Meteorological Organization, January 10, 2025, https://wmo.int/news/media-centre/wmo-confirms-2024-warmest-year-record-about-155degc-above-pre-industrial-level. I have experienced the rail problem several times myself, when Amtrak trains in the American southeast were delayed for hours because of heat.
3. Note that human abilities to tolerate high wet bulb conditions may have been overstated. Katie Bohn, "Humans Can't Endure Temperatures and Humidities as High as Previously Thought," Penn State, March 1, 2022, https://www.psu.edu/news/story/humans-cant-endure-temperatures-and-humidities-high-previously-thought/. For air quality, see "Atrocious Air," First Street, February 12, 2024,

https://firststreet.org/research-library/atrocious-air. For air turbulence, see Carissa Wong, "Singapore Airlines Turbulence: Why Climate Change Is Making Flights Rougher," *Nature*, May 22, 2024, https://www.nature.com/articles/d41586-024-01542-2. Bryan Alexander, "Academia in the Storms' Path: The New Hurricane Season," blog, October 9, 2024, https://bryanalexander.org/climatechange/academia-in-the-storms-path-the-new-hurricane-season/.

4. "The Insurance Issue," First Street, n.d., https://pitch.com/v/Insurance-Bubble-cihncu/c21522cf-b860-46aa-a4f7-461ae6af1d63; Erin C. Pettit, Christian Wild, Karen Alley et al., "Collapse of Thwaites Eastern Ice Shelf by Intersecting Fractures," AGU21 Fall Meeting, New Orleans and online, December 15, 2021, https://agu.confex.com/agu/fm21/meetingapp.cgi/Paper/978762; Clare Trapasso, "Climate Risks Threaten Nearly Half of All Homes in the U.S.: What Buyers and Sellers Need To Know," Realtor.com, March 13, 2024, https://www.realtor.com/news/trends/climate-risks-threaten-nearly-half-of-all-homes/.
5. Michael B. Mahon, Alexandra Sack, O. Alejandro Aleuy et al., "A Meta-Analysis on Global Change Drivers and the Risk of Infectious Disease," *Nature* 629 (2024): 830–836, https://www.nature.com/articles/s41586-024-07380-6; Robin Foster, "FDA Approves Vaccine to Prevent Infection with the Chikungunya Virus," UPI, November 10, 2023, https://www.upi.com/Health_News/2023/11/10/FDA-vaccine-chikungunya-virus/8071699627394/; Nils B. Tjaden, Jonathan E. Suk, Dominik Fischer, Stephanie M. Thomas, Carl Beierkuhnlein, and Jan C. Semenza, "Modelling the Effects of Global Climate Change on Chikungunya Transmission in the 21st Century," *Scientific Reports* 7, no. 3813 (2017), https://doi.org/10.1038/s41598-017-03566-3; "First Human Case of Emerging Tick-Borne Disease Reported in Northeast," Yale School of Public Health, September 30, 2024, https://ysph.yale.edu/news-article/first-human-case-of-emerging-tick-borne-disease-reported-in-northeast/.
6. Everett M. Rogers, *Diffusion of Innovations*, 5th ed. (Simon and Schuster, 2003).
7. Bill McKibben, "Tesla, Big Oil Have a Weakness in Common: They're Way Behind the Technological Curve," *The Crucial Years*, Substack, March 21, 2025, https://billmckibben.substack.com/p/tesla-big-oil-have-a-weakness-in.
8. Michael E. Mann, "Welcome to the American Petrostate," *Bulletin of Atomic Scientists*, November 7, 2024, https://thebulletin.org/2024/11/welcome-to-the-american-petrostate/.
9. Nancy M. Sidun and Judith L. Gibbons, "Women, Girls, and Climate Change: Human Rights, Vulnerabilities, and Opportunities," *International Journal of Psychology* 59, no. 2 (2023): 257–266, https://doi.org/10.1002/ijop.12942; Matthias Berninger, "Climate Change Impacts Women More. We Must Legislate to Protect Their Health," World Economic Forum, January 16, 2024, https://www.weforum.org/stories/2024/01/women-health-climate-change/.
10. One ex-academic offers a passionate call for academics to act against collapse: Rupert Read, "Ecologism or Barbarism," *Brave New Europe*, November 16, 2023, https://braveneweurope.com/rupert-read-ecologism-or-barbarism.

6. Academia and the Struggle for Humanity's Future

Epigraph: Marc Andreessen, "The Techno-Optimist Manifesto," Andreesen Horowitz, October 16, 2023, https://a16z.com/the-techno-optimist-manifesto/; Edward Abbey, *The Journey Home: Some Words in Defense of the American West* (Penguin, 1991).

1. Ian Morris, *Why the West Rules—For Now: The Patterns of History, and What They Reveal About the Future* (Farrar, Straus and Giroux, 2010). The appendix is especially useful concerning metrics. J. Bradford DeLong, *Slouching Towards Utopia: An Economic History of the Twentieth Century* (Basic Books, 2022); "How Capitalism Revolutionized the Way We Live, and How Economics Attempts to Understand This and Other Economic Systems," CORE Economics, https://www.core-econ.org/the-economy/v1/book/text/01.html#eb-17; "This Is How Many Humans Have Ever Existed, According to Researchers," World Economic Forum, April 4, 2022, https://www.weforum.org/stories/2022/04/quantifying-human-existence/; Luke Muehlhauser, "Three Wild Speculations from Amateur Quantitative Macrohistory," blog, September 12, 2017, https://lukemuehlhauser.com/three-wild-speculations-from-amateur-quantitative-macrohistory/; Luke Muehlhauser, "How Big a Deal Was the Industrial Revolution?" blog, n.d., https://lukemuehlhauser.com/industrial-revolution/.
2. One useful account of progress flagging is Tyler Cowen, *The Great Stagnation: How America Ate All the Low-Hanging Fruit of Modern History, Got Sick, and Will (Eventually) Feel Better* (Dutton, 2011).
3. Caleb E Finch, "Evolution of the Human Lifespan and Diseases of Aging: Roles of Infection, Inflammation, and Nutrition," *Proceedings of the National Academy of Sciences* 107, supplement 1 (January 26, 2010): 1718–24, https://doi.org/10.1073/pnas.0909606106; Centers for Disease Control, "Life Expectancy." n.d., https://www.cdc.gov/nchs/fastats/life-expectancy.htm (That data reminds us of a strong gender difference, with men's lifespan averaging 74.8 years while women reach 80.2 years). See also excellent visualization by Saloni Dattani, Lucas Rodés-Guirao, Hannah Ritchie, Esteban Ortiz-Ospina, and Max Roser, "Life Expectancy," OurWorldinData, 2023, https://ourworldindata.org/life-expectancy. "Zeroth world" is quite underdiscussed; I assembled some references and notes at Bryan Alexander, "What Is the Zeroth World, and How Can We Use It?," blog, October 10, 2019, https://bryanalexander.org/futures/what-is-the-zeroth-world-and-how-can-we-use-it/.
4. Antong Zhang, Jiani Yang, Yangcheng Luo, and Siteng Fan, "Forecasting the Progression of Human Civilization on the Kardashev Scale Through 2060 with a Machine Learning Approach," *Scientific Reports* 13, no. 11305 (2023), https://doi.org/10.1038/s41598-023-38351-y.
5. Cixin Liu, *Death's End*, trans. Ken Liu (Tor, 2016).
6. Alvin Toffler, *The Third Wave* (William Morrow, 1980); Aaron Bastani, *Fully Automated Luxury Communism: A Manifesto* (Verso, 2019). Alvin Toffler received publishing credit, but futurists now see Heidi Toffler as co-creator of the works under his name. Kevin Kelly, "Extropy," *The Technium* (blog), August 29, 2009,

https://kk.org/thetechnium/extropy/. A classic text here is Ray Kurzweil, *The Age of Spiritual Machines: When Computers Exceed Human Intelligence* (Viking, 1999).

7. Toby Ord, *The Precipice: Existential Risk and the Future of Humanity* (Grand Central Publishing, 2021) offers a good example of longtermist thinking. See also William MacAskill, *What We Owe the Future* (Basic Books, 2022).
8. Émile P. Torres, "The Dangerous Ideas of 'Longtermism' and 'Existential Risk,'" *Current Affairs*, July 2021, https://www.currentaffairs.org/news/2021/07/the-dangerous-ideas-of-longtermism-and-existential-risk; Timnit Gebru and Émile P. Torres, "The TESCREAL Bundle: Eugenics and the Promise of Utopia Through Artificial General Intelligence," *First Monday* 29, no. 4 (2024), https://doi.org/10.5210/fm.v29i4.13636.
9. Andreessen, "Techno-Optimist Manifesto." We can find an echo of that population boom idea in Matthew Yglesias, *One Billion Americans: The Case for Thinking Bigger* (Penguin, 2020).
10. Full credit for the name "Demodern" goes to Dickinson College professor and good friend Ed Webb.
11. Bill McKibben, *Falter: Has the Human Game Begun to Play Itself Out?* (Henry Holt, 2019).
12. Naomi Klein, *This Changes Everything: Capitalism vs. The Climate* (Simon & Schuster, 2014).
13. Frank White, *The Overview Effect: Space Exploration and Human Evolution*, 3rd ed. (American Institute of Aeronautics and Astronautics, 2014): Jordan Bimm, "Rethinking the Overview Effect," *Quest* 21, no. 1 (2014): 39–47.
14. Donna Haraway, *Staying with the Trouble: Making Kin in the Chthulucene* (Duke University Press, 2016).
15. Kate Raworth, *Doughnut Economics: Seven Ways to Think Like a 21st-Century Economist* (Random House, 2017); Herman E. Daly, *Beyond Growth: The Economics of Sustainable Development* (Beacon Press, 1996); "What is a Circular Economy?" United States Environmental Protection Agency, n.d., https://www.epa.gov/circulareconomy/what-circular-economy; "Circular Economy: Definition, Importance and Benefits," European Parliament, May 24, 2023, https://www.europarl.europa.eu/topics/en/article/20151201STO05603/circular-economy-definition-importance-and-benefits.
16. One clear introduction is Jason Hickel, Giorgos Kallis, Tim Jackson et al., "Degrowth Can Work—Here's How Science Can Help," *Nature*, December 12, 2022, https://www.nature.com/articles/d41586-022-04412-x; Kohei Saito, *Slow Down: The Degrowth Manifesto*, trans. Brian Bergstrom (Astra, 2024).
17. William J. Ripple, Christopher Wolf, Detlef P. van Vuuren, Jillian W. Gregg, and Manfred Lenzen, "An Environmental and Socially Just Climate Mitigation Pathway for a Planet in Peril," *Environmental Research Letters* 19, no. 2 (2024), https://iopscience.iop.org/article/10.1088/1748-9326/ad059e.
18. Tim Jackson, *Prosperity Without Growth: Foundations for the Economy of Tomorrow*, 2nd ed. (Routledge, 2016); Dietrich Vollrat, *Fully Grown: Why a Stagnant Economy Is a Sign of Success* (University of Chicago Press, 2020); Giacomo D'Alisa, Federico

Demaria, and Giorgos Kallis, eds., *Degrowth: A Vocabulary for a New Era* (Routledge, 2015); Jakub Kronenberg, Erik Andersson, Thomas Elmqvist, Edyta Łaszkiewicz, Jin Xue, and Yaryna Khmara, "Cities, Planetary Boundaries, and Degrowth," *The Lancet* 8, no. 4 (2024), https://www.thelancet.com/journals/lanplh/article/PIIS2542-5196(24)00025-1/fulltext.

19. The Overshoot Day project gives a good introduction at https://overshoot.footprintnetwork.org/; William E Rees and Mathis Wackernagel, "The Shoe Fits, but the Footprint is Larger than Earth." *PLoS Biology* 11, no. 11 (2013), https://doi.org/10.1371/journal.pbio.1001701.
20. For one chilling account of atomic catastrophe, see Annie Jacobsen, *Nuclear War: A Scenario* (Dutton, 2024).
21. Vanessa Machado de Oliveira, *Hospicing Modernity: Facing Humanity's Wrongs and the Implications for Social Activism* (Penguin, 2012).
22. Dougald Hine, *At Work in the Ruins: Finding Our Place in the Time of Science, Climate Change, Pandemics and All the Other Emergencies* (Chelsea Green, 2023); "What Should Academics Do About Climate Change?" posted January 27, 2023, by Bryan Alexander, YouTube, 58 min., 41 sec., https://youtu.be/t_uHLuKgXrs?si=te53A4k4sy1pJgoT; Alexandra Alter, "A Sci-Fi Writer Returns to Earth: 'The Real Story Is the One Facing Us,'" *New York Times*, May 11, 2022, updated June 22, 2023, https://www.nytimes.com/2022/05/11/books/kim-stanley-robinson-sci-fi.html; "CACOR Live—Ruben Nelson Meta Challenge of the 21st Century," posted March 5, 2025, by Canadian Association for the Club of Rome, YouTube, 105 min., 54 sec., https://youtu.be/zMReVieFyTw?si=iw6EkRe5QkyeGyeW; Kim Stanley Robinson, *Aurora* (Orbit, 2015); "The End of Globalisation and the Return of Localisation—Rupert Read's Keynote Lecture," posted Oct 30, 2019, by Rupert Read, YouTube, 74 min., 52 sec., https://youtu.be/JxIdhv2KHb8?si=s31WBRCUScYGilze. See also Thomas W. Murphy, Jr, *Energy and Human Ambitions on a Finite Planet* (University of San Diego Open Education Resources, 2021), https://doi.org/10.21221/S2978-0-578-86717-5.
23. Monica Byrne, *The Actual Star* (Harper Voyager, 2021); Robert Silverberg, "The Wind and the Rain," in *Unfamiliar Territory* (Berkeley, 1973), 202–3. Astonishingly, a yogurt commercial offers a clear and inspiring solarpunk vision—see "'Dear Alice' Decommodified Edition | Solarpunk Anime Ambience with No Ads," Posted October 19, 2021, by Waffle to the Left, YouTube, 1 min., 19 sec., https://www.youtube.com/watch?v=UqJJktxCY9U&ab_channel=WaffleToTheLeft.
24. Noah Smith, "Degrowth: We Can't Let It Happen Here! We Won't Help the Environment or the Poor by Valorizing Poverty and Decline," *Noahpinion*, Substack, May 23, 2023, https://www.noahpinion.blog/p/degrowth-we-cant-let-it-happen-here; Donella H. Meadows, Dennis L. Meadows, Jørgen Randers, and William W. Behrens, *Limits to Growth: The 30-Year Update* (Potomac Associates—Universe Books, 1972); Charles C. Mann, *The Wizard and the Prophet: Two Remarkable Scientists and Their Dueling Visions to Shape Tomorrow's World* (Knopf, 2018); Paul Sabin, *The Bet: Paul Ehrlich, Julian Simon, and Our Gamble over Earth's Future* (Yale University Press, 2014).

25. Vegard Skirbekk, *Decline and Prosper!: Changing Global Birth Rates and the Advantages of Fewer Children* (Palgrave Macmillan, 2022); Klaus Æ. Mogensen, "Mars is Irrelevant to Us Now. We Should of Course Concentrate on Maintaining the Habitability of the Earth," Farsight, August 10, 2022, https://farsight.cifs.dk/interview-kim-stanley-robinson/.
26. Marc Andreessen, "The Techno-Optimist Manifesto," Andreesen Horowitz, October 16, 2023, https://a16z.com/the-techno-optimist-manifesto/.
27. For decolonization, see the remarks by Dr. Oscar Mwaanga in "Decolonizing Higher Education," posted August 30, 2024, by Bryan Alexander, YouTube, 54 min., 47 sec., https://youtu.be/6rjaeh--A4g?si=hUf_Ho43bAny3pvF.

7. *Managed Descent*

Epigraphs: Sheridan Hendrix, "Ohio Public Universities Face Massive Budget Cuts. Here's What's At Risk," *Columbus Dispatch*, March 14, 2024, https://www.dispatch.com/story/news/education/2024/03/14/ohio-public-universities-face-multimillion-dollar-budget-cuts/72757439007/; Ryan Anderson, "The Warning Signs of Academic Layoffs," *Inside Higher Ed*, August 20, 2024, https://www.insidehighered.com/opinion/career-advice/2024/08/20/how-prepare-and-protect-your-career-against-layoffs-opinion.

1. Sharon Otterman, "Facing Budget Troubles, Some Colleges Look to Sell the President's House," *New York Times*, last updated February 20, 2024, https://www.nytimes.com/2024/02/16/nyregion/new-school-presidential-residence-sale-budget-troubles.html; William Westhoven, "Bid to Preserve Drew University Forest Hits Snag as Judge Rules in School's Favor," *Morristown Daily Record*, March 14, 2025, https://www.dailyrecord.com/story/news/local/morris-county/2025/03/14/nj-judge-throws-wrench-into-plan-to-preserve-drew-university-forest/82272488007/; Brian Boucher, "'It Defames Me': Brauer Museum Founding Director Blasts Valparaiso University's Ongoing Deaccessioning Plan," Artnet, July 1, 2024, https://news.artnet.com/art-world/brauer-museum-founding-director-response-valparaiso-university-2506372.; Milla Surjadi, "Classroom Weddings, Riding Lessons: The New College Campus Moneymakers," *Wall Street Journal*, July 27, 2024, https://www.wsj.com/us-news/education/classroom-weddings-riding-lessons-the-new-college-campus-moneymakers-22870d16.
2. Ben Unglesbee, "Johnson & Wales University to Lay Off 91 Faculty and Staff," *Higher Ed Dive*, May 8, 2025, https://www.highereddive.com/news/johnson-wales-university-91-layoffs-faculty-staff-deficit/747604/; Juliet Schulman-Hall, "Clark U. Was Booming 3 Years Ago. How They Got to Laying Off 30% of Faculty," MassLive, June 4, 2025, https://www.masslive.com/news/2025/06/clark-u-was-booming-3-years-ago-how-they-got-to-laying-off-30-of-faculty.html.
3. Robert C. Dickeson, *Prioritizing Academic Programs and Services: Reallocating Resources to Achieve Strategic Balance* (Jossey-Bass, 2010).
4. Benjamin Ginsberg, *The Fall of the Faculty* (Oxford University Press, 2011); Josh Moody, "How Sweet Briar College Defied the Odds of Closure," *Inside Higher Ed*, March 27, 2025, https://www.insidehighered.com/news/governance/executive

-leadership/2025/03/27/how-sweet-briar-college-defied-odds-closure; Alander Rocha, "Alabama House Repeals Financial Lifeline Program Intended for Birmingham-Southern College," *Alabama Reflector*, April 26, 2024, https://alabamareflector.com/2024/04/26/alabama-house-repeals-financial-lifeline-program-intended-for-birmingham-southern-college/.

5. Ben Unglesbee, "Cal Maritime and Cal Poly Set to Merge," *Higher Ed Dive*, November 22, 2024, https://www.highereddive.com/news/cal-maritime-cal-poly-merger-California-State-University-Academy-Polytechnic/733794/; Lola Duffort, "Merger Between Marlboro College and University of Bridgeport Unravels," *VTDigger*, September 14, 2019, https://vtdigger.org/2019/09/14/merger-between-marlboro-college-and-university-of-bridgeport-unravels/.
6. Tressie McMillan Cottom, *Lower Ed: The Troubling Rise of For-Profit Colleges in the New Economy* (The New Press, 2018)
7. Mark Lungariello, "Sold! Masons' $32M Bid for College of New Rochelle Campus Approved in Bankruptcy Court," lohud, last updated December 18, 2019, https://www.lohud.com/story/marketplace/real-estate/2019/11/25/college-of-new-rochelle-bankruptcy-auction-sale/4299972002/; Michael Rodriguez, "Guest Post: College Closures and the Implications for Libraries and Vendors," Scholarly Kitchen, September 5, 2024, https://scholarlykitchen.sspnet.org/2024/09/05/college-closures/.

   An *Insider Higher Ed* series that offers a good example of a closure process: Helen Drinan, Michelle Filling-Brown, and Richie Gebauer et al., "Closing With Dignity," *Inside Higher Ed*, February 19, 2025, https://www.insidehighered.com/opinion/views/2025/02/19/closing-college-dignity-part-1-opinion; Helen Drinan, Michelle Filling-Brown, and Richie Gebauer et al., " No Good Time to Close a University," *Inside Higher Ed*, February 26, 2025, https://www.insidehighered.com/opinion/views/2025/02/26/closing-college-dignity-part-2; Jennifer N. Suriano, Terri Ward, and Julienne Cuccio Slichko, "Our College Closed: Advice for Navigating Professional Deaths and Rebirths," *Inside Higher Ed*, April 8, 2025, https://www.insidehighered.com/opinion/career-advice/advancing-faculty/2025/04/08/after-closure-professional-deaths-and-rebirths.
8. John Luciew, "Penn State Trustees Cast 'Painful' Vote to Close 7 Campuses: 'New Course for Next Century,'" *PennLive*, last updated May. 23, 2025, https://www.pennlive.com/pennstate/2025/05/penn-state-trustees-casts-painful-vote-to-close-7-campuses-new-course-for-next-century.html.
9. Rebecca Griesbach, "Birmingham-Southern College Closing May 31 as Loan Bill Fails to Gain Support: 'This Is a Tragic Day,'" AL.com, last updated March 27, 2024, https://www.al.com/educationlab/2024/03/birmingham-southern-college-will-close-may-31-as-loan-bill-fails-to-gain-support.html.
10. Ricardo Azziz, "Why Is the Higher Education Sector So Fragile in the US? The Answer Lies in How Colleges and Universities First Developed Across the Country, According To One Consolidation Expert," *Higher Ed Dive*, August 19, 2024, https://www.highereddive.com/news/merger-watch-us-fragile-higher-education/724471/.

11. Sara Weissman, "A Pennsylvania Community College Campus Closes In-Person Programs," *Inside Higher Ed*, March 6, 2025, https://www.insidehighered.com/news/quick-takes/2025/03/06/pa-community-college-campus-closes-person-programs.
12. Dick Startz, "Are Colleges Really Facing an Enrollment Cliff?" Brookings Institution, October 17, 2024, https://www.brookings.edu/articles/are-colleges-really-facing-an-enrollment-cliff/.
13. Elizabeth Hewitt, "The Other Victims When Colleges Decline or Close: Their Hometowns," *Hechinger Report*, February 12, 2019, https://hechingerreport.org/the-other-victims-when-colleges-decline-or-close-their-hometowns/; Amy Scott and Sofia Terenzio, "When Colleges Close, Communities Take the Biggest Hit," Marketplace, February 17, 2025, https://www.marketplace.org/story/2025/02/17/when-colleges-close-communities-take-the-biggest-hit.
14. John Warner, *Sustainable, Resilient, Free: The Future of Public Higher Education* (Belt, 2020).
15. Susan H. Greenberg, "2 University System of Georgia Institutions to Merge," *Inside Higher Ed*, April 17, 2025, https://www.insidehighered.com/news/quick-takes/2025/04/17/two-university-system-georgia-institutions-merge.
16. One example of academic dishonesty appears in this dark short story: E. Saxey, "Not Smart, Not Clever," Apex Book Company, May 6, 2014, https://www.apexbookcompany.com/a/blog/apex-magazine/post/not-smart-not-clever.
17. Interestingly, climate fiction has been exploring this kind of geoengineering effort. See, for example, the Apple TV series *Extrapolations* (2023) or Neal Stephenson's novel *Termination Shock* (HarperCollins, 2021).
18. "U.S. Higher Education Outlook 2025," Fitch Ratings, December 3, 2024, https://www.fitchratings.com/research/us-public-finance/us-higher-education-outlook-2025-03-12-2024; Ben Unglesbee, "Moody's Turns Negative on Higher Ed's Financial Outlook Amid Trump Cuts," *Higher Ed Dive*, March 19, 2025, https://www.highereddive.com/news/moodys-negative-outlook-higher-ed-trump-cuts/743014/.
19. Douglas-Gabriel, interview.

8. Climbing Back to Peak

Epigraph: Myles Horton, Paulo Freire, and Brenda Bell, *We Make the Road by Walking: Conversations on Education and Social Change* (Temple University Press,1990), 218.

1. The Google AI NotebookLM offered these observations about this chapter in its podcast feature: "It's not about accepting decline. . . . It's about finding new paths forward. . . . It can be unsettling, but also a chance for something new, something better. . . . The peak might be behind us, but that doesn't mean the descent has to be a crash. It can be a chance to rebuild, to reimagine, and even a chance to rediscover the power of education in a world that desperately needs it."
2. Nathan M. Greenfield, "Coalition Unites Around Need for More International Students," *University World News*, November 10, 2023, https://www.universityworldnews.com/post.php?story=20231110093836586.

3. Rachel Scholten, "Could the US Benefit from the International Student Backlash Elsewhere?" *University World News*, July 20, 2024, https://www.universityworldnews.com/post.php?story=20240717141423969.
4. Natalia Orlova, Derek Rury, and Justin C. Wiltshire, "Out-of-State Enrollment, Financial Aid and Academic Outcomes: Evidence from Wisconsin," EdWorking-Paper 23–840 (Annenberg Institute, Brown University, September 2023), https://doi.org/10.26300/skvw-0v45; Peter D'Auria, "At Vermont's Flagship Public University, Growing Out-of-State Enrollment Prompts Questions About Its Mission," *VTDigger*, September 7, 2023, https://vtdigger.org/2023/09/07/at-vermonts-flagship-public-university-growing-out-of-state-enrollment-prompts-questions-about-its-mission/.
5. See this powerful critique of OPMs: Kevin Carey, "The Creeping Capitalist Takeover of Higher Education," Highline, *HuffPost*, April 2019, https://www.huffpost.com/highline/article/capitalist-takeover-college/.
6. Interview with Doug Shapiro, National Student Clearinghouse.
7. Government Accounting Office (GAO), *Higher Education: Students Need More Information to Help Reduce Challenges in Transferring College Credits*, GAO-17-574, August 2017, https://www.gao.gov/assets/gao-17-574.pdf; Kyle Gray, Betsy Mueller, Emily Tichenor, and Madeline Joy Trimble, "Holistic Credit Mobility Strategies in Action: A Case Study Report on State, System, and Institutional Efforts to Smooth the Path to a College Degree for Mobile Students," Ithaka S+R, February 27, 2025, https://doi.org/10.18665/sr.322216; Charles M. Ambrose and Michael T. Nietzel, *Colleges on the Brink: The Case for Financial Exigency.* (Rowman & Littlefield, 2023), 194–6.
8. Bryan Alexander, *Universities on Fire: Higher Education in the Climate Crisis* (Johns Hopkins University Press, 2023); Zenaida Kotala Gonzalez, "CU Denver Launches Psychedelic Research Center in Downtown Denver," press release, June 24, 2024, https://news.ucdenver.edu/university-of-colorado-denver-launches-psychedelic-research-center/; "Graduate Studies in Medical Cannabis," University of Maryland School of Pharmacy, n.d., https://www.pharmacy.umaryland.edu/academics/graduate-studies-in-medical-cannabis/; "Cannabis Studies Majors," Roanoke College, n.d., https://www.roanoke.edu/academics/majors/cannabis_studies.
9. "Characteristics of Postsecondary Students," National Center for Education Statistics (NCES), updated August 2023, https://nces.ed.gov/programs/coe/indicator/csb/postsecondary-students; "Student Enrollment: How Many Students Ages 25 and over Enroll in Postsecondary Institutions in the Fall?" National Center for Education Statistics (NCES), n.d., https://nces.ed.gov/ipeds/trendgenerator/app/trend-table/2/8?trending=column&rid=59; "Today's Students," Lumina Foundation, 2024, https://www.luminafoundation.org/campaign/todays-student/.
10. Allison Beer, "Diversity of Community College Students in 7 Charts," Association of Community College Trustees, n.d., https://perspectives.acct.org/stories/diversity-of-community-college-students-in-7-charts; "Fast Facts From Our Fact Sheet," American Association of Community Colleges, n.d., https://web.archive.org/web/20150723145013/http://www.aacc.nche.edu/AboutCC/Pages/fastfactsfactsheet

.aspx; Sarah Damaske and Adrianne Frech, "The Myth of Men's Full-Time Employment," *The Conversation*, February 8, 2024, https://theconversation.com/the-myth-of-mens-full-time-employment-221078; Zsófia L. Bárány, Pauline Corblet, and Moshe Buchinsky, "Older-Adult College Enrollment Trends and Benefits," Brookings Institution, February 26, 2024, https://www.brookings.edu/articles/older-adult-college-enrollment-trends-and-benefits/; "Some College, No Credential Student Outcomes 2024 Report for the Nation and the States," National Student Clearinghouse Research Center, June 6, 2024, https://nscresearchcenter.org/some-college-no-credential/; Karin Fischer, "'That Ship Has Sailed': For Many of America's 40 Million College Dropouts, the Reasons Not to Return Are Obvious," *Chronicle of Higher Education*, February 15, 2024, https://www.chronicle.com/article/that-ship-has-sailed.

11. "Uncharted Territory A Guide To Reimagining Higher Education," Stanford University Design School, n.d., https://dschool.sfo3.digitaloceanspaces.com/documents/Uncharted-Territory-Stanford-2025-Part-Two-digital-guide.pdf.
12. One example of posted tuition cuts: Kathryn Palmer, "Tuition Resets Continue Amid Public Skepticism of College's Value," *Inside Higher Ed*, September 15, 2023, https://www.insidehighered.com/news/business/revenue-strategies/2023/09/15/amid-skepticism-colleges-value-tuition-resets-keep. One good survey of free college programs: Alcino Donadel, "About 370 More Free College Programs Have Erupted Nationwide in 8 Years," *UB: University Business*, July 13, 2023, https://universitybusiness.com/about-370-more-free-college-programs-have-erupted-nationwide-in-8-years/?oly_enc_id=6911B4589589A9Z; Jenny Brundin, "Free College in Colorado? It's Covered if You're Interested in Teaching, Firefighting, Law Enforcement, Construction or Forestry," Colorado Public Radio, July 18, 2023, https://www.cpr.org/2023/07/18/colorado-free-college-career-advance-program/.
13. Taylor K. Odle and Jennifer A. Delaney, "You are Admitted! Early Evidence on Enrollment from Idaho's Direct Admissions System," *Research in Higher Education* 63 (January 31, 2022): 899–932, https://doi.org/10.1007/s11162-022-09675-x; Scott Jaschik, "For Direct Admissions Pioneers, It's a Good Year," *Inside Higher Ed*, May 1, 2023, https://www.insidehighered.com/news/admissions/traditional-age/2023/05/01/direct-admissions-pioneers-its-good-year; "VCU Announces Guaranteed University Admission Program," press release, Virginia Commonwealth University, October 4, 2023, https://news.vcu.edu/article/2023/10/vcu-announces-guaranteed-university-admission-program.
14. Sylvia Casacuberta Puig and The Crimson Editorial Board, "High Time to End Legacy Admissions," editorial, *Harvard Crimson*, October 28, 2021, https://www.thecrimson.com/article/2021/10/28/high-time-to-end-legacy-admissions/; Carolyn Jones, "California Banned College Legacy Admissions. Will It Change Who Gets In?" *CalMatters*, October 18, 2024, https://calmatters.org/education/higher-education/2024/10/college-admissions-2/.
15. Eric Mazur has a wealth of information at his site, https://mazur.harvard.edu/research-areas/peer-instruction. This is a good case study of one campus strategically making active learning work at scale. See also our Future Trends

Forum conversation with Mazur, "Active Learning After a Pandemic Year," posted August 26, 2021, by Bryan Alexander, YouTube, 55 min., 13 sec., https://youtu.be/PJ-sfCnJCMY?si=OeFTVC1-vohzmExp; Beckie Supiano, "Can This University Change Its Teaching Culture?" *Chronicle of Higher Education*, March 8, 2024, https://www.chronicle.com/article/can-this-university-change-its-teaching-culture; Elli J. Theobald, Mariah J. Hill, Elisa Tran, et al., "Active Learning Narrows Achievement Gaps for Underrepresented Students in Undergraduate Science, Technology, Engineering, and Math," *PNAS* 117, no. 2 (2020), https://doi.org/10.1073/pnas.1916903117; Kevin A. Nguyen, Maura Borrego, Cynthia J. Finelli et al., "Instructor Strategies to Aid Implementation of Active Learning: A Systematic Literature Review," *International Journal of STEM Education* 8, no. 9 (2021), https://doi.org/10.1073/pnas.1916903117.

16. *How People Learn: Brain, Mind, Experience, and School*, expanded ed. (National Academies, 2000); *How People Learn II: Learners, Contexts, and Cultures* (National Academies, 2018); Joshua R. Eyler, *How Humans Learn: The Science and Stories behind Effective College Teaching* (West Virginia University Press, 2018).
17. Mary C. Wright, *Centers for Teaching and Learning: The New Landscape in Higher Education* (Johns Hopkins University Press, 2023).
18. Neil Selwyn, *Education and Technology: Key Issues and Debates* (Bloomsbury Academic, 2021). The most recent edition includes a great deal of criticism. Jenna Joo, Deanna Marcum, and Daniel Rossman, "CIC Consortium for Online Humanities Instruction II: Evaluation Report for the Second Course Iteration," Ithaka S+R, September 19, 2018, https://sr.ithaka.org/publications/cic-consortium-for-online-humanities-instruction-ii-2/; Bryan Alexander, "The American Experience in Vietnam: Notes on the Design and Teaching of a Multi-Campus, Interdisciplinary, Computer-mediated Course," Insights feature article, Technology: Tool or Method?, 2002, https://web.archive.org/web/20130613011300/https://toolormethod.wlu.edu/insights.html; Seymour Papert, *Mindstorms: Children, Computers, and Powerful Ideas* (Basic Books,1980) is a fountainhead. The EDUCAUSE group is possibly the world's leading organization for accumulating information and networking people on this topic: https://www.educause.edu/.
19. "Undergraduate Degree Earners Academic Year 2023–24," National Student Clearinghouse Research Center, April 10, 2025, https://nscresearchcenter.org/undergraduate-degree-earners/.
20. Keil Dumsch has been a steady thinker and activist on this theme.
21. "Is College Worth It?: Black, Latinx, and Indigenous Student Voices on the Value of Postsecondary Credentials A Comprehensive Education Report," The Pell Institute, 2024, https://www.pellinstitute.org/wp-content/uploads/2024/11/COE_Pell-Institute_Lumina-PELL_PostSecondaryValue_Report_v-12B.pdf.
22. Richard V. Reeves, *Of Boys and Men: Why the Modern Male Is Struggling, Why It Matters, and What To Do About It* (Brookings Institution Press, 2022).
23. Journalist and professor Nikole Hannah-Jones urged all Black students to attend HBCUs, arguing that predominantly white institutions (PWIs) could not

sufficiently support them. Remarks at the American Association of Colleges and Universities conference, January 2025.

24. David Scobey, "The Paradigm Project: A Call for Radical Renewal of Higher Education," *Change*, March/April 2023, https://www.tandfonline.com/doi/epdf/10.1080/00091383.2023.2180274?needAccess=true.

25. "Bringing It #129: More Remedies for Exhaustion: Responses to the Current Threats, BT2P's Changemakers Network, and a New Job Opportunity," BT2P: Bringing Theory to Practice, February 6, 2025, https://bttop.org/bringing-it-129-more-remedies-for-exhaustion-responses-to-the-current-threats-bt2ps-changemakers-network-and-a-new-job-opportunity/; Oliver Morrison, "Amid Enrollment Decline, Pittsburgh-Area Colleges Ponder Combined Operations as Way to Save," 90.5 WESA, September 28, 2023, https://www.wesa.fm/education/2023-09-28/college-enrollment-decline-pittsburgh-robert-morris-carlow-chatham-point-park-washington-jefferson; "Cost-Saving Initiatives," New York Six Liberal Arts Consortium, n.d., https://newyork6.org/cost-saving-intiatives; Joo, Marcum, and Rossman, "CIC Consortium"; Roger Schonfeld, *JSTOR: A History* (Princeton University Press, 2003); James L. Shulman, *The Synthetic University: How Higher Education Can Benefit from Shared Solutions and Save Itself* (Princeton University Press, 2023).

INDEX

Browse more books from **HOPKINS PRESS**

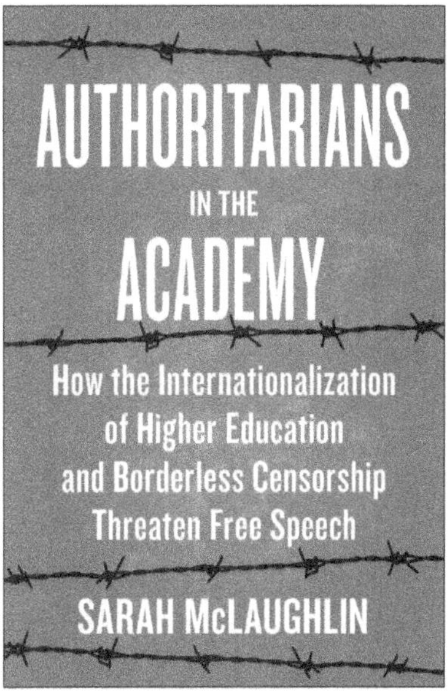

JOHNS HOPKINS UNIVERSITY PRESS | PRESS.JHU.EDU